Northern Tales No. 5

Whimsical Memories of "North Country Boy"

by Jerry Harju

Northern Tales No. 5

Whimsical Memories of "North Country Boy"

by Jerry Harju

Cover Design by Stacey Willey
Edited by Karen Murr and Pat Green

Copyright 2009
Jerry Harju

Published by North Harbor Publishing
Marquette, Michigan

Publishing Coordination by
Globe Printing, Inc.
Ishpeming, Michigan

Printed by Thomson-Shore, Inc, Dexter, Michigan

ISBN 0-9788898–2-7
Library of Congress Control Number 02008911958

February 2009

No portion of this publication may be reproduced, reprinted, or otherwise copied for distribution purposes without express written permission of the author and publisher.

INTRODUCTION

I began my writing career with a series of autobiographical, short-story books on the perils (not fatal, but comical) of growing up in Michigan's Upper Peninsula. They were "Northern Reflections," "Northern D'Lights," and "Northern Passages." Humorous stuff yet giving the reader a pretty good idea of what life was like in the U.P. back then. Later I added "Northern Memories." I've written other books as well, but people keep asking when I plan to write another book in the "Northern" series. Well, here it is.

Over the years I've found that some of my readers like the short-story format of the "Northern" books, and others like the essay format of other books of mine. In an attempt to keep everyone happy, "Northern Tales No. 5" has both short stories and essays.

The tales hearken back to the late 1930's, '40's and '50's, when I was growing up and going off to college.

The photograph on the cover was taken in 1938 at my cousin Karen Murr's 3rd birthday party in Ishpeming, Michigan. She's the cute one in the white dress. The others are cousins Barbara Engstrom, Elmer Maki, and his younger brother Eugene. I hate to admit it, but I'm the one with the pained expression wearing knickers held up by the silly suspenders. It wasn't my best photo opportunity. Enjoy the book.

Jerry Harju
North Harbor Publishing
528 E. Arch St.
Marquette, MI 49855
Toll Free (877) 906-3984
E-mail: jharju@chartermi.net
Website: www.jerryharju.com

DEDICATION

To my parents, to whom I owe everything.

ACKNOWLEDGMENTS

As I've mentioned in my other books, putting a book together requires the time and expertise of several very talented people. I especially thank my long-time editors, Karen Murr and Pat Green, who once again put the final professional polish to my writing. Stacey Willey did an excellent job on the cover design and page layout. Joan Antilla and Alice Eman, my high-school classmates, provided very timely research material on our senior year. Once again Steve Schmeck was kind enough to produce the bar codes for the cover.

Books and CD by Jerry Harju

NORTHERN REFLECTIONS
NORTHERN D'LIGHTS
NORTHERN PASSAGES
NORTHERN MEMORIES
NORTHERN TALES NO. 5
THE CLASS OF '57
COLD CASH
HERE'S WHAT I THINK...
WAY BACK WHEN
OUR WORLD WAS IN BLACK & WHITE
THE WITCHES PICNIC (CD)

CONTENTS

A Christmas Recitation 9

The Old Man 13

Remembering Mom 27

Days of Wine and Tulips 31

A True Crime Story 35

Food We Never Ate 53

Kids Going to War 57

A Time For Model Building 61

A Position of Authority 65

When Dumps Were Dumps 85

The Science of Downhill Skiing 89

Senior Year 93

College Girls 101 111

Biography 137

A CHRISTMAS RECITATION

In 1938 I was a five-year-old rookie in the Bethel Lutheran Church Sunday School in Ishpeming. Sunday School was nice. We sat there and listened to Bible stories and then had cookies and milk during the final minutes. In early December we began singing Christmas carols. Mrs. Maki, the Sunday School teacher, sat at the old upright piano in the church basement, clunked out a few chords, and led us in the carols. We were too young to read so she'd go over each verse several times to help us learn the words.

At that age I had a sponge-like brain and memorized all the carols with no problem. It even surprised Mrs. Maki, and one Sunday she mentioned it to my mother after the Sunday church service. She suggested to my mother that it would be utterly charming if I stood up and recited the 23rd Psalm from memory at the Christmas Eve service. The congregation would be quite impressed to see someone so young reciting the psalm.

My mother thought it was an excellent idea and told me about it at home.

"Whut's the 23rd Psalm?" I asked.

She explained that it was a beautiful prayer, and the congregation would love to hear me reciting it.

"I gotta do this in front of everybody in church?"

"You're so good at learning things by heart that it'll be easy."

So, for the next two weeks I was drilled incessantly on the 23rd Psalm. Over and over again. I even learned how to pronounce 'righteousness' without tripping over my tongue.

At 6PM on Christmas Eve I rattled off the psalm five or six times while my mother helped me get dressed. I still had trouble tying my shoes, but I had the 23rd Psalm down cold.

That evening every pew in the church was filled. My parents were seated in the back, but because I was in the program I was in the first pew. My 15-year-old sister, Esther, was in the choir and sitting right behind me.

It came to my turn, and I marched up front and center. My mother had told me that since the 23rd Psalm was a prayer it was okay to close my eyes while I recited it. That way I wouldn't get distracted by the congregation.

It was good advice, and that's exactly what I did. With eyes shut I began reciting the psalm. It started off fine.

Then I made a fatal blunder. I opened my eyes and looked directly at my sister in the second pew.

Now, Esther was the perfect role model for a younger brother. She was getting all A's in high school, never stayed out late, helped my mother around the house, and never complained about what was on her plate at dinner time. My mother thought she was an absolute angel.

I knew better.

Esther had a goofy side that few people ever saw, but when the two of us were alone she'd frequently give me a dose of it. She'd start by contorting her face in a way that would have made Harpo Marx envious. Once she had me giggling she'd start tickling me until tears were streaming down my face, and I'd be gasping for breath. Then she'd walk away as if nothing happened.

So that Christmas Eve in the Bethel Lutheran Church, facing

hundreds of people, I had the bad fortune to open my eyes and look in her face just after I'd begun my recitation.

With a deadpan expression, Esther slowly crossed her eyes.

The words of the psalm began flopping around in my brain, randomly rearranging themselves. I immediately shut my eyes, hesitated, and picked up the psalm, although I may have dropped a line or two.

"Yea, though I walk through the valley of the shadow of death . . ."

I compulsively opened my eyes again. Now Esther had twisted her face around to look like the Hunchback of Notre Dame, tongue flopping around in her open mouth like a beached fish.

I began giggling. Everyone knows that the valley of the shadow of death is no place to giggle, but I couldn't help it, it just popped out. Somehow, though liberally interspersed with suppressed giggles, hiccups, and stammering I got through the psalm and stumbled back to my seat.

After the program people came up, patted me on the head, and told me what a great job I did. But I knew they were just trying to make me feel better. All my mother said was, "What was wrong with you?"

Right then I almost ratted on my sister, but it wouldn't have done any good. My mother never would have believed that Esther would do such a thing.

I trudged home in a deep depression. Mom offered me a slice of buttered saffron bread, my Christmastime favorite food. I didn't want any. I didn't want to stay up to catch Santa Claus. I just wanted to go to bed.

The next morning I woke up still dwelling on my botched recitation. But hey, it was Christmas morning, and there might be presents under the tree.

I went downstairs. There it was under the tree, the present of my dreams. Weeks ago Gately's in Ishpeming had opened a Christmas toy department, and that's where I spotted it. I told my father that I really hoped Santa Claus would bring it to me. The old man just said, "It cost five dollars! Santa Claus don't have that kind'a money!"

But now it was under our tree, a fully equipped, exactly to scale Standard Oil gas station! Two pumps with real rubber hoses, and–are you ready for this?–exact-replica Standard Oil bulbs on top of the pumps that were lighted! And that wasn't all–inside there was a lube hoist that went up and down by turning a crank! This was turning out to be a wonderful Christmas after all.

My mother again offered me a slice of buttered saffron bread. I took a big bite. It tasted just great.

THE OLD MAN

My first memory of the old man–my father–was sitting on his lap when I was two years old. He had a distinctive smell that my mother didn't have, my sister didn't have, or the dog didn't have. I found out later that the smell was from the horses. Paddy and Dick were draft horses the old man used for the field work on the family potato farm west of Ishpeming. He had no use for any mechanized device that ran on wheels so he didn't have a tractor. He never drove or owned a car either.

I would sit on his lap right after supper (dinner was eaten at noon) when he'd smoke his after-supper cigarette. First the cigarette had to be rolled. The old man would reach into his shirt pocket and pull out a packet of Zig Zag cigarette papers, wet his thumb and peel off a sheet. Out came the bag of Bull Durham tobacco, and he'd delicately sprinkle a line of tobacco flakes across the Zig Zag sheet.

The tricky part was rolling it into a cylinder, licking the gummed edge of the paper to seal it, and twisting the ends shut. Now it was ready to smoke. If I never ever did anything else in my life, I had to learn how to roll a cigarette. And I wanted to smell like the old man.

☙❧

My father never yelled at me. He gave me advice but quietly and seriously. And he didn't waste his breath telling me something more than once. His philosophy was that if I didn't listen to him the first time, then let the consequences be my guide. Naturally, I had to learn that the hard way.

Back then my grandmother–Mummu Harju–lived on Superior Street in Ishpeming. In her back yard was a large barn where she kept cows and chickens as well as Paddy and Dick.

The barn had a hay loft, and one day when I was about four–just old enough to climb the ladder–the old man let me go up into the loft to play in the hay. He climbed up with me and pointed at square holes cut into the loft floor where he pitched hay down into the feed bins. "Stay away from them holes," he warned. "Ya might fall down there on a cow or a horse."

Did I listen to him? Of course not. Every day I climbed into the loft to play, and naturally I'd venture over to the holes and peer down at Paddy's and Dick's heads. I had no interest in cows.

One day I was near the edge of a hole and lost my balance. The next thing I knew I was hanging in midair, my fingers frantically clutching the edge of the hole with my feet dangling a few feet above Paddy's ears.

The huge draft horse gazed up at me, his head several times the size of my entire body. My heart galloped up into my throat. I was going to fall into the feed bin and *BE EATEN BY A GIANT HORSE!* I screamed bloody murder.

In seconds the old man was up the ladder and plucked me out of the hole. He looked me over to make sure I was okay and then went back down the ladder to resume his chores. No yelling or saying "I told you so." In fact, he didn't say a word. I never went near those holes again.

ഈര

The Old Man

In the fall of 1941, about the time my father gave up growing potatoes, my mother landed a good-paying job as a seamstress at the Gossard Company in Ishpeming. One drawback: I was only eight years old, and someone needed to see that I was dressed, had breakfast, and got off to school on time. My sister Esther—ten years older—had already gone off to college. Guess who got stuck with the job.

The first morning the old man was in charge I came downstairs and sat down at the kitchen table.

"Whaddaya want for breakfast?" he asked.

"Pancakes!" I shouted. This was going to be great. I loved pancakes. My mother never *asked* what I wanted for breakfast; it was always yucky, hot oatmeal during the school year, whether I liked it or not.

The old man rooted around among the pots and pans and came up with the biggest frying pan he could find. He threw a couple of logs into the kitchen stove and put the frying pan on top to heat while he attempted to figure out how to make pancake batter. After reading the instructions on the Aunt Jemima box he poured the ingredients into a big bowl and stirred. The result didn't resemble pancake batter whatsoever. A powdery scum floated on the surface with large lumps popping up here and there. He finally decided it would be simpler to make just one pancake, so he poured all the batter into the large frying pan.

The pancake came out the size of a manhole cover but thicker. It was black and hard on the bottom and white and pasty on top. Syrup puddled on it like an oil slick. It didn't taste very good, but the old man kept watching to see how I liked it, so I ate the whole thing.

That evening my mother asked me what I'd had for breakfast.

"A pancake," I said.

Knowing how much I loved pancakes, she was suspicious. "Only one?"

"One was enough."

The next day when I came home for lunch my father had already heated up some Campbell's chicken noodle soup.

"Ya want anything else?" he asked.

"Can I have some toast, too?"

He tossed two slices of bread on top of the wood stove. When the bread started to smoke he turned them over and did the other side. The burnt toast looked terrible, but with butter and jam it wasn't half bad.

I was never very particular about what I wore to school, and the old man didn't worry about it either. One day the third-grade teacher looked at my mismatched socks and asked who had dressed me that morning.

"I dress myself," I said with pride. However, not wanting to take full credit, I added, "My father helps me a little bit, though."

The teacher nodded and then asked where my mother was.

One day the old man decided that I should help him keep the house straightened up. He showed me how simple it was.

"Ya just put everything outta sight," he said. To demonstrate his point he picked up yesterday's *Mining Journal* off the carpet and jammed it into the library-table drawer. That didn't look too hard, I thought, so I went around the house and did the same thing. The house looked pretty good to both of us.

As the days went by my mother kept finding odd things in odd places: a toy fire truck in with my clean underwear, a dirty coffee cup in the refrigerator vegetable bin, a dog bone in a kitchen drawer. She realized that having the old man in charge of the home front wasn't working out. She managed to get her Gossard schedule adjusted so she could be at home in the morning to inspect my clothes, make my breakfast, and see me off to school. Things drifted back to normal, and I didn't see pancakes for breakfast for a long while.

☙❧

The Old Man

One spring my mother decided that she wanted new wallpaper in the living room, or front room as we called it back then. She was about to hire a professional paperhanger when the old man butted in.

"Why spend all that money," he said. "Wallpapering is easy. We kin do it ourselves and save a bundle."

A few days later all of the front-room furniture had been pushed into the kitchen or out into the yard. A couple of saw horses with planks across them took center stage in the bare room. My parents were ready to start wallpapering, although my mother had reservations about it.

The first order of business was the ceiling paper. To save even more money the old man decided to make his own paste, mixing flour and water. When he began spreading it on the back of the paper my mother pointed out that the paste was too lumpy. He said it'd be just fine after he smoothed out the paper up on the ceiling.

An hour later the few lonely strips of new paper sticking to the ceiling looked as though several large chipmunks had gotten trapped underneath. My mother was loudly announcing that the paste was still too lumpy. The old man, hair now liberally decorated with white pasty lumps, began defending his handiwork using very salty language. My mother shooed me outside.

I snuck back into the house in order not to miss the action. The old man was struggling to stick another pasted strip to the ceiling and just about had it fastened in place when the paper broke loose, landing with a splat on top of his head. The soggy paper split apart and settled onto both of his shoulders.

Right then Mummu Harju walked in and witnessed the whole thing. I never found out exactly what she said to my father because she was yelling in Finn, but he quickly tore the ceiling paper off his body and scrambled to the floor. The next day a professional paperhanger came in and finished the job.

My father really loved Christmas. It would begin in early December when he would tell my mother, "Hey, time to go out and get a Christmas tree, eh?" And she'd always say, "Now, don't bring one back that's too big."

The old man would get hold of one of his friends who had a car and we'd pile in and go out to the woods and start the search. Invariably he'd spy one about 14 feet tall. His eyes would light up, and he'd chop it down and tie it to the top of the car. We'd get it home and he'd bring it into the front room and try to stand it up. My mother would yell, "You did it again! Too big! Saw some off the bottom." The old man would get a saw and cut four or five feet off the base of the tree. It was a family tradition, and it happened every year.

My father loved games at Christmas. My presents from Santa provided him with a perfect excuse to get down on the living-room rug and show off his skills. Tiddlywinks was his favorite. The game is simple in principle but next to impossible to play well. Tiddlywinks is played on the rug using a glass cup and brightly colored, nickel-sized disks called winks. The object of the game is to get a wink into the cup by pressing down on the edge of one wink with another, causing it to flip into the air. Simple, right? Wrong. You have absolutely no idea where the wink will go. It can take a feeble little hop and go nowhere, or fly off sideways and scoot under the sofa, or zoom straight up and hit you between the eyes. When the dog saw us taking out the Tiddley Winks game he'd take cover.

My old man was the champion, though. He could put those winks into the cup with astonishing regularity. I couldn't understand how he did it because he never played Tiddleywinks any other time of year.

ಸುಂ

The one thing my father wasn't able to succeed at was teaching me to be a deer hunter. In the fall of 1948 I was fifteen years old and

The Old Man

looking forward to my first deer season. But I was facing it without a deer rifle. I had shown the old man the Winchester 30-30 carbine in the new Sears catalog, and he immediately asked where the $35 was going to come from to pay for it.

I was prepared for this, pointing out that we could send Sears four dollars and they would send the rifle. But my father demanded full disclosure, and I had to admit that Sears would expect four dollars every month thereafter for a year. He quickly did the math and asked me why I thought it made sense to pay $48 for a $35 rifle. In his way of thinking, buying things on credit ranked right up there with politics. He didn't understand either one.

But the deer-rifle dilemma was resolved. From a top shelf in his bedroom closet the old man hauled out an old khaki duffle bag with a shoulder strap. It held an ancient rifle. The butt stock was dull and scarred, and the long barrel was streaked with rust. A sliding wood handgrip was attached to a cylindrical magazine beneath the barrel. It was my father's pump-action .32 caliber rifle that he'd had since before World War I.

The old man handed me a single cartridge for the rifle. "The only one I got. It's a .32 Remington rimless. Don't see 'em around anymore. Better get started lookin' for some. Might be hard to find."

A mammoth understatement. Clem Hooper ran a combination hardware and sporting goods establishment and was the undisputed arms expert in Republic. He inspected my cartridge like it was a rare Mesopotamian coin . He had never seen the likes of it. Fortunately a week later my uncle Hugo located a box of twenty of the rare .32 Remington rimless for the unheard sum of six dollars. I had to use up half my life's savings to buy ammunition.

With the old rifle and ammunition in hand the old man led me to an old gravel pit outside of Republic where he put up a 2-foot-diameter white target. At 100 yards away it looked like a B-B, but my father sighted in the rifle and effortlessly plunked a shot almost dead center on the target. Then he handed me the Remington. After several seriously errant shots I managed to nick the edge of the target. The old man now realized that when it came to shooting I must have taken after my mother, but since we'd now used up half of the precious ammunition he reluctantly nodded his approval. I was marginally ready for deer season.

The day before opening day my father took me to the Republic cemetery. He pointed at deer tracks in the powdery snow at the south edge of the property. "This buck's been crossing through here every morning regular as clockwork. If ya sit in that rock outcropping in the middle of the cemetery you'll get a good shot at him." Then he added, "Two things to remember. When you get in those rocks don't move around. And if the wind's blowin' up your back from the north you might as well come home cause he'll smell ya a mile off."

The next morning before sunup I was stationed in the rock outcropping. The weather was bitterly cold but too early for my long underwear and winter cap with ear flaps. I needed full flexibility with my trigger finger so I didn't wear gloves.

Pale November morning light slowly gave definition to the tombstones. I huddled in the rocks, turning blue from the north wind blowing icy spears up the back of my jacket. The metal magazine of the rifle felt like a popsicle on my bare left hand. The tips of my ears were getting numb.

Two hours crept by and the buck didn't show. I had to get up and move around or die. Mummu Olander, my maternal grandmother, lived 200 yards from the cemetery gate. I could almost smell the strong, hot coffee that she always had in a big pot on her wood stove in the morning. And the ever-present sweet rolls on the table. What the hell, a fifteen-minute break wouldn't make a big difference in my luck. I scrambled out of the rocks and took off.

A half hour later, totally thawed out by three cups of coffee and stoked up with sweet rolls and a slice of jelly roll I strolled back into

The Old Man

the cemetery.

The tracks of the buck were fresh in the snow.

He had crossed the cemetery while I was drinking coffee. If I had looked out of my grandmother's kitchen window, I would have seen him. Only then did I realize that the icy wind that had frozen my spine was coming from the north, from me to the deer. He had waited until I left.

When I got home I screwed up my courage and told my father what had happened. The old man just nodded his head and said nothing.

❧

Months later I was absorbed with a totally different priority. I wanted a car. I approached the old man about this, knowing that it was going to be a replay of the deer-rifle confrontation only much, much tougher. He didn't have a car stashed away in an old duffel bag, and since he had no use for cars he certainly wasn't inclined to buy one for me.

But hope springs eternal, and I brought up the subject one night at supper.

"Ya want a car? Whut for?" The old man's intent was to convince me that a car was a totally frivolous luxury, and I could find much more sensible ways to spend my money.

But I pointed out that I could do the grocery shopping at the Red Owl store and haul the bags home in my car. With a car I could also deliver my grandmother's mail on the other side of town instead of the old man having to make the journey on foot every morning. My mother was listening to the conversation, and I could tell that I was making a good case, but she kept her mouth shut.

My father saw that he wasn't going to talk me out of it so he issued his final statement on the subject. "Ya wanna car so bad you'll hafta earn every dollar to pay for it!" He knew he was on safe ground.

My parents were running a restaurant in Republic and paid me five dollars a week to help out after school and on weekends. But that money was always spent feeding my raging addiction to Cokes and candy bars. The old man was certain that I'd never be able to get the sugar monkey off my back so there would be no money saved.

But he grossly underestimated my desire for a car. I began saving money with a frenzy. The weekly five-dollar wage from the restaurant got squirreled away in a bank in my bedroom. I cut way back on Cokes and candy bars, and when I *REALLY* had to have a sugar fix I'd weasel a quarter out of my mother. When my sister sent me birthday money it got saved. When my mother asked what I wanted for Christmas I said, "Money."

My uncle Arvid began giving me driving lessons in his war-surplus oversized jeep vehicle. It had four-wheel drive and required double clutching to shift gears, but once I mastered that big hunk of iron I knew I could drive anything.

One morning in May, 1949 I approached my father sitting at the kitchen blowing on a saucer of hot coffee.

"I got $120. Enough to buy a car."

The old man almost dropped the saucer into his lap. "Whut?"

"I said, I got $120 and I want to buy a car."

After gathering his wits he replied, "Well, if yer gonna do it, I'm gonna help ya pick it out."

Days later we were in Ishpeming looking at a '32 Chevy coupe. One of my high-school buddies had mentioned that a friend of his in Ishpeming had his car up for sale.

The coupe was a thing of beauty with white sidewall tires, a nice fluffy fox tail mounted on the radio aerial, and a pair of fuzzy pink dice tied to the rear-view mirror. The kid wanted $125 for it, but I was certain that he'd take the $120 I had in my pocket.

"It's too fast," the old man said.

I stared at him in astonishment. "Whaddaya mean, too fast?"

"It's too fast."

It's parked. The car's not moving. How can you say it's too fast?"

"It's too fast." That was the end of the '32 Chevy coupe.

What did I wind up with? A 1930 Model A Ford with a tall boxlike chassis, vertical windshield, and powered by a spunky little four-cylinder engine which, when idling, sounded like a panting dog on a hot day. A car not built for speed. The important thing was that the old man had given it his blessing.

The supreme irony was that I no sooner bought the Model A when the old man developed a passion for riding in it. He suddenly had a need to visit every relative we had in Republic, and we had quite a lot of them. He still delivered the morning mail to my grandmother, but now he wanted to ride there.

It all evened out, though. Whenever the old man got in the car the first stop we always made was the Standard station where I'd hit him up for gas money.

෫෨෬෭

The final confrontation I had with my father was also the one that had the most profound impact on my life. In January, 1951 the two of us were driving to Marquette in the Model A. I was going there to take a scholarship exam for the University of Michigan. I didn't want to take this exam since I had big plans after high school to go to Milwaukee and make some big money. But my mother was having none of that, so I was going to take the exam. The old man was tagging along to make sure I did it. On the road we had something like the following conversation.

"You know," I said. "I hear them tool'n die makers down in Milwaukee are making *eight* dollars an hour."

The old man said, "Y'think ya can just go t'Milwaukee an' be a tool'n die maker? It'd take ya longer t'learn *that* than gettin' a college degree."

"Mebbe, but at least I'd be getting a paycheck while I'm learning."

"Look, ya got plenty a time later t'worry 'bout money. We'll get ya through college somehow. Don't forget, we still got them war bonds t'cash."

"Look," he said. "Four more years a school ain't gonna hurt ya. Then, anyway–with a college degree–ya kin pick and choose from a better class of work."

"What do *you* know 'bout college?" I said hotly. "You didn't even get through the sixth grade." I immediately regretted saying that, knowing he'd had to quit school to go to work.

The old man barked out a laugh. "Well, yer right about that. I don' know nuthin' 'bout college, or any kind'a education, fer that matter.

Tell ya whut I *do* know sumthin' about, though. *No* education! *No* education is hitchin' up a team a horses out in the woods before the sun comes up and it's twenty-five below–like it is this mornin'–but ya can't go inside an' warm up 'cause ya haf'ta drag logs 'cross the snow all day. *No* education is sweatin' yer ass off all summer growin' potatoes that nobody kin buy, an' ya wind up givin' 'em away or tradin' 'em fer somethin' else t'eat 'cause yer tired of eatin' potatoes alla time. *No* education is havin' t'mop up the mess when some drunken pulp-cutter staggers into th'restaurant late at night and throws up on yer clean floor. Ask me anythin' ya want 'bout *no* education, boy. I'm a damned expert on that!"

We continued the trip in silence, but the old man's descriptions of the work he'd done in his lifetime were so graphic that it chilled my bones. I took the exam in Marquette, was awarded four years of scholarship at Michigan, and went on to get a degree in engineering. I've attributed it all to that one conversation we had on the way to Marquette in my Model A.

The Old Man

※

After college I wound up in California working in the aerospace industry. During the 1960's and '70's my parents would occasionally take the Greyhound bus out to the West Coast to visit and I in turn would fly back to Michigan from time to time to see them. Then in 1984 my mother called and said, "Pop isn't doing too well." I immediately flew to Michigan and picked up my mother in Republic. We drove to Ishpeming to see my father in the Mather Nursing Facility.

Old age and heart trouble hadn't treated the old man kindly. At 89 he was thin and withered and spoke in a quiet, shaky voice. But he hadn't lost his sly smile and sense of humor. We spoke of many things, mostly mundane topics, but when I got up from his bedside to leave he put his hand on my arm and said, "Y'know, y'turned out okay. I'm proud of you." He had never said that before.

A month later the most brilliant man I ever had the privilege to know–a man who never made it through the sixth grade–passed away. I'll always miss him.

※

REMEMBERING MOM

When I was young I was convicted life would have been much easier if my mother hadn't been involved. Later, of course, I realized that I was very lucky she had been around.

Today's young mothers seem to cling more and more to the belief that sitting down with your children and reasoning with them is the most effective method of teaching the difference between right and wrong.

My mother knew that trying to reason with someone whose brain was only half-developed (namely me) was a complete waste of time. She was more a practitioner of Newton's Third Law: the law of reciprocal actions. If I committed a kid crime, she dished out the punishment. This cause-and-effect rule was easy to understand and didn't employ a lot of complex logic involving morality.

Her preferred punishment was grabbing my hair and pulling me straight up, standing me on my tiptoes. While she was doing this she explained why it was happening and then asked if I understood. I had to give a verbal reply because it's hard to nod your head while hanging by your hair. I'd have more hair today if I hadn't screwed up so much when I was a kid.

So, as I was growing up my mother pretty much dictated how

things were going to be. At the dinner table what I would eat was never a subject for debate. If I said–and I remember saying just that–"Ma, I don't like cooked carrots," she'd give me her patented icy stare which meant, that's too bad because then you'll be unhappy while you're eating them.

We never discussed what I was going to wear either. Nowadays kids tell their mothers what clothes they want, depending on what their friends are wearing. Nothing like that ever happened at our house. Every August before school started Mom would buy my yearly wardrobe–without consulting me, of course–from the Sears & Roebuck or Montgomery Ward catalogs or drag me down to Penney's in downtown Ishpeming. When I put on a new pair of pants that she picked out we always had the following conversation.

"They're too big, Ma."

"Never mind. You'll grow into them."

There was only one day in the year when my clothes fit perfectly. Before that day they were too big, and afterward they were too small.

My mother was a strict disciplinarian, but she also had a benevolent side. She used every opportunity to get me educated. When I was four years old I showed a keen interest and aptitude for jigsaw puzzles. Mom bought me a jigsaw puzzle map of the United States where each puzzle piece was a state. I loved the puzzle and put it together over and over. To this day I still have a sharp mental image of U. S. geography.

When I was in the first grade and began reading she took my hand, walked me to the Ishpeming Carnegie Library and introduced me to the children's-book section. I was soon making the library trip by myself, and I've been an avid reader ever since.

My sister, Esther, became an excellent piano player at an early age. I was seven years old when my mother told me that I was going to follow in Esther's footsteps and start taking piano lessons. "No, no, I don't wanna take piano lessons!" I cried.

Remembering Mom

"Shut up! You're gonna take piano lessons. Some day you'll thank me."

So, for four years I took piano lessons and hated it. But a strange thing happened. In my late twenties I fell in love with folk music, bought myself a guitar, and began taking lessons. Amazingly, it came easy, mainly because I still remembered musical scales, keys, and chords from my early piano days. I went on to teach folk guitar for many years. Mom was right again.

In the following decades my mother and I locked horns on many issues, and this continued even when she was well into her eighties.

Then in 1996, after a 38-year engineering career in California, I retired and moved back to the U. P. My father had passed away in 1984, and Mom, now 95, was a nursing-home resident in Ishpeming. Arthritis and old age had bent and shriveled her body, and she looked nothing like the active, robust mother I had known from long ago. She had now given up telling me what to do. Instead on my daily visits she would greet me with a warm, gentle smile which always conveyed to me that she was saying, okay, I've done my best. Now you're on your own.

Your best was pretty darn good, Mom. I'm proud and privileged to be your son.

☙❧

DAYS OF WINE AND TULIPS

The following took place before I was born. My mother was 80 years old when she told me the story. It took her 60 years to finally be able to laugh about it.

In 1925 my parents had just bought a house on South Second Street in Ishpeming. My father was raising potatoes on a small farm north of town, but this was the Depression, and the market for potatoes was nil. My sister, Esther, was just a toddler. With a small baby, paying cash for the house, and practically no income, the wolf was growling at the door.

The country was in the throes of Prohibition, but the ban on the legal sale of alcoholic beverages had little effect on preventing a large segment of the American public from drinking. And as you might guess, the U.P. was no exception. Prohibition bootleggers thrived up here. They made any kind of booze that people were willing to pay for. For a few coins you could buy "beer," "whiskey," "gin," or "wine," vintaged last week, all neatly packaged in a plain brown paper bag.

My father observed that many of the Italians in our neighborhood were raking in a tidy profit making and selling wine. He had a brilliant idea. If they could do it, why not him? Finns were just as smart as Italians.

The initial task, though, was selling the idea to my mother. When he brought up the subject she threw a fit.

"Making wine in our house? Never! What will the ladies in the Lutheran sewing circle say when they hear that federal agents broke down our door? You must be touched in the head!"

But the old man kept after her. Okay, it's a little illegal, but what's the harm? Half the people in Ishpeming are doing it, and the cops are just looking the other way. Then he threw out his most compelling argument. He slyly pointed out that selling wine would provide them with extra spending money. She might even be able to afford more flowers for the garden.

Flowers were my mother's sole vice. That spring she'd mailed in a hefty order to Montgomery Ward for petunia and marigold seeds and tulip bulbs. Now he was using the tulips as leverage.

You have to understand that they'd only been married a short time, and my mother was still under the illusion that the old man knew everything about everything. She finally went along with the wine-making project, convinced that it would be a safe, profit-making venture.

The old man got busy. He was going to make chokecherry wine since there were several chokecherry trees in our yard. The root cellar beneath the kitchen was nice and cool, ideal for the purpose. He hauled an old pickle crock down the ladder into the root cellar, filled it with water and ripe chokecherries, added sugar and yeast, and placed a towel over the top of the crock.

My mother, being an experienced cook, became interested in the wine-making process and followed his progress. My father explained that the fermentation process was now taking place, and over a period of several weeks all there was to do was stir the contents of the crock twice a day.

The summer wore on. Every morning before he left for the farm, the old man would go down into the root cellar and stir the crock. He repeated the procedure when he returned late in the afternoon.

Days of Wine and Tulips

Then one day my mother realized that she hadn't seen him climbing down into the root cellar for several days. But it was hay-harvesting time at the farm, and with all that work he'd probably just forgotten. She decided to help out and stir the crock herself. She climbed down into the root cellar and turned on the light.

The crock was empty.

Judging from the number of cigarette butts on the dirt floor and the tin cup next to the empty crock, it was apparent that the old man had fallen in love with his product.

It didn't take a team of federal agents to shut down the notorious South Second Street bootlegging operation. My mother did that singlehandedly. The family did make some money on Prohibition, however. Years later my sister would scour the alleys for empty bottles to sell to the bootleggers so she could afford the Saturday matinee at the Ishpeming Theater.

༺༻

A TRUE CRIME STORY

Imogene Poppingail, a girl in my fourth-grade class at Central School in Ishpeming, came up to me on the playground during recess.

"I hear you collect stamps," she said.

"Yeah," I said carefully, edging away. I always avoided contact with Imogene. She was the class intellectual, having read every volume of the Bobbsey Twins, and she had the unsettling habit of telling you something you didn't know but were supposed to know.

"I collect stamps too," she said. "How big is your album?"

"Album? What's an album?"

"Don't you have an album to keep your stamps in?"

"I keep 'em in a cigar box."

Imogene looked at me with astonishment. "A cigar box? You're not a stamp collector at all."

"Whaddaya mean? Sure I am."

"You have to keep them in an album—a book for your stamps. Didn't you know that? All stamp collectors have albums. Some albums are so big that they have pages for stamps from every country in the world."

"Yer makin' that up."

"No, I'm not. Ask the teacher."

"So where do I get this album?"

"Newberrys has them."

"What do I do, glue the stamps on the pages?"

Imogene was astounded at my ignorance. "Glue? Boy, you don't know anything about stamp collecting. You put the stamps on the pages with hinges."

"Hinges?" I said, thinking of door hinges. "What kind'a baloney is that?"

Imogene decided to take pity on me, explaining that hinges were little pieces of gummed paper used to affix the stamps to the page. Then she added, "First you soak the stamps in water to get them off the envelopes. I suppose you didn't know *that* either."

In defense of my lack of stamp-collecting knowledge I replied, "I only been collecting for a month."

Up to a month ago collecting stamps had never entered my mind. In 1943 World War II was raging, and many other urgent projects were on my agenda. Being a fierce home-front patriot, my bedroom walls were festooned with European and Pacific maps and silhouettes of every known enemy aircraft. I collected scrap iron and tin foil. Every week I faithfully purchased one defense stamp from my teacher at school. I even enjoyed oleo on my sandwiches, as opposed to people who thought that being forced to eat oleo instead of butter was the cruelest atrocity that Germany and Japan had committed

My Uncle Arvid was in the army and sending me letters from Europe, fascinating reading even though Army censors industriously blotted out every other word. Then, with one of the letters, Arvid included a matching set of British postage stamps in the envelope. There were six of them, each stamp a different color and denomination, all with side-by-side portraits of Queen Victoria and King George. They were beautiful. I put the stamps in a cigar box where I kept my really valuable stuff, like the Captain Midnight secret decoder ring and things like that.

A True Crime Story

From that day on I was a stamp collector.

A few days later a mail-order package from Montgomery Ward arrived with my new school clothes. The brown wrapping paper had three stamps of different U.S. presidents. I ignored the school clothes and cut the stamps off the paper.

I began looking for stamps everywhere. As a Depression baby, I had a natural talent for prowling the Ishpeming alleys, pawing through garbage cans for anything of value. Trash proved to be a rich source of stamps, although many of them had to be wiped clean of coffee grounds.

☙❧

I decided that Imogene was right; I needed a stamp album. I checked out the albums at Newberrys, and the one I had to have—an all-world album—cost two dollars. Fortunately, my mother was very supportive of this new hobby, reasoning that stamp collecting was a far more refined pastime than iron-ore battles with the Catholic kids from across the tracks. She gave me two dollars.

Leafing through the album at home I was stunned by the number of nations listed on the pages, places I'd never heard of like Gambia, Bechuanaland, Dahomey, Grenada, Barbuda, Guadeloupe, Swaziland, and Zanzibar. Where was I going to get stamps from these pipsqueak countries? I mounted my stamps in the album, but my meager little collection sunk out of sight in the vast array of blank pages.

I needed another source of stamps.

☙❧

Then one Saturday at the Ishpeming Library I was thumbing through the latest copy of *Open Road for Boys*. On a back page was the following ad.

> STAMPS
> Expand your stamp collection with our beautiful worldwide issues—mint and used. Mailed to you on approval.
> SEND NO MONEY.
> Jolly Badger Stamp Company
> 203 Wells St, Milwaukee, Wisconsin

Send no money. My first encounter with that insidiously seductive phrase. I glanced at the librarian, making sure she wasn't watching and then quietly ripped the ad from the magazine.

Two weeks later I received a thick packet from the Jolly Badger Stamp Company. It was full of stamps. The enclosed letter read:

> *Dear Mr. Harju:*
>
> *As a new client, welcome! You are invited to inspect the enclosed stamps, many of which we are certain will become valuable additions to your collection. The price is listed below each stamp. Make your selections and enclose the payment in the return envelope along with the remaining stamps. Again, our sincere welcome! We look forward to doing business with you in the future. Yours very truly,*
>
> *The Jolly Badger*
> *Stamp Company*

At least one hundred stamps were hinged to several pages—strange exotic stamps from all over the world. One from Afghanistan had a portrait of a dark, brooding, bearded man wearing a fez, like Major Hoople in the comics. "Deutsches Reich" was imprinted on another. I wouldn't have had a clue where it came from except for the picture of Adolph Hitler sporting a swastika armband. An Italian stamp of Mussolini—jaw thrust out—facing Hitler. I *had* to have that one. Stamps with monkeys, lions, and penguins. A triangular stamp from Costa Rica. I wanted them all.

On the last page I found a stamp where the phrase "I want" was not adequate. I *HAD* to have this stamp! The stamp literally popped my eyeballs out of their sockets. It was a Cuban stamp with a nude woman lying on a couch, a picture of a painting no doubt done by some famous Cuban artist. But that fact was totally lost on me. All I knew was that *I could buy a stamp with a totally naked woman on it!*

With shaking fingers I removed the stamp from the sheet.

I went back and looked again at all of the sheets. After restraining myself—plucking off only the stamps that I couldn't live without—I added up what I owed the Jolly Badger Stamp Company. It totalled ninety-five cents.

I didn't get a weekly allowance, so I had to bum nickels and dimes from my father to cover the usual expenses: Saturday matinees, candy, ice cream, and the occasional ten-cent comic book. It was an extremely good week if I managed to talk him out of fifty cents. Trying to hit up the old man for ninety-five cents to buy stamps that couldn't even be used to mail letters would have been sheer folly.

In my bedroom I had a savings bank, a repository over the years for money gifts from Christmas and my birthday. The savings bank was exactly that, for savings. I had been given strict orders never to touch the money. In fact, all I ever did was insert coins and the occasional bill into a slot in the top of the bank. It was my money but I had no say on how it would eventually be spent.

The bank had a combination lock, and I wasn't even supposed to know how to open it, but I had found out the combination. I opened the bank and took out ninety-five cents. I'd replace it later I told myself.

☙❧

I sent the money and the remainder of the stamps to the Jolly Badger Stamp Company in the conveniently supplied return envelope. Ten days later I received another packet of stamps with a letter.

> *Dear Mr. Harju:*
> *Thank you for the prompt remittance for your selections from our first approval set. You will be pleased to know that we have now upgraded your customer status to "preferred". Preferred customers can review our highest-grade stamps, many of which we have included in this mailing.*
> *Very truly yours*
> *The Jolly Badger Stamp Company*

The stamps in this envelope included a set of sixteen five-cent U.S. stamps, each with a different multicolored flag of an occupied country in Europe–Poland, France, Norway, etc: I carefully removed them from the sheet. There were others. A set from Germany–Adolph Hitler scowling fiercely from beneath the bill of a high-peaked military cap, a Nigerian stamp with a threatening open-mouthed hippopotamus, a Costa Rican stamp with a brilliant yellow pineapple.

I totalled up what I owed. One dollar and forty cents. I paid another visit to my savings bank.

※

Weeks later, I took the album to school to show it to Imogene during recess. I casually turned the album pages at my desk as she watched over my shoulder. When I got to the Cuba page I paused, letting Imogene get a good gander at the only Cuban stamp in my collection. I heard a small squeak as she sharply sucked in her breath.

"It's only a painting," I remarked casually, illustrating that I had indeed become a man of the world and a sophisticated stamp collector.

"Where did you get . . . uh . . .all these stamps?" she gulped.

"I bought them," I informed her.

"You *bought* them?"

"Sure. They're sent to me from Milwaukee." I explained the approval arrangement with the Jolly Badger Stamp Company, who had now elevated my customer status from "preferred" to "prime."

"You have so many from other countries." She pointed at one page. "Helvetia–where's that?"

"Helvetia is Switzerland in the Switzerland language," I explained patiently. All world stamp collectors should know that, I thought, but I didn't say anything to Imogene. No point rubbing it in. My newly acquired philatelic knowledge was the result of evenings at the Ishpeming Library studying the 1943 Scott Stamp Catalog.

                                ಸಂಐ

A packet of approval stamps came from The Philatelic Wonders Stamp Company in Baltimore. I hadn't ordered them and couldn't understand how they knew that I collected stamps. At age ten I knew nothing about the trading of mailing lists between companies. Philatelic Wonders had sent some fabulous stamps, though, and I picked some out and sent in the money.

A few days later I received stamps from the Collector's Delight Stamp Company in St. Louis, Missouri. They sent me an extensive selection of U.S. commemoratives. I selected several, took a dollar and a quarter from my bank, and started a third account.

By now I had become quite adept at mounting stamps with paper hinges, and the pages in my album were becoming dotted with exotic stamps.

                                  ಸಂಐ

Even though I'd carefully avoided telling my parents about the approval transactions, my mother noticed that I was receiving more mail than the rest of the family combined.

"What's in all of those fat letters from stamp companies?" she asked.

"Well, companies send me stamps on approval. If I see a stamp I like, I take it for my collection and send them the money."

My mother got right to the crux of the matter. "How much are you spending on those stamps?"

"Oh . . . not much . . . just a few pennies and nickels." In fact, it was quite a few pennies and nickels, but I wasn't keeping track. Every time an approval packet arrived in the mail I'd just pay another visit to my little bank.

"Can I see your collection?"

I brought out the album and leafed through some of the pages while my mother looked over my shoulder. I took great care to avoid the Cuba page.

Satisfied, my mother said, "Well, don't overdo it."

☙❧

No one in our family had ever received mail from California, but one day I got an approval packet of airmail stamps from a place called Air-Post Treasures in Los Angeles. The only airmail stamp I had in my collection had been rescued from the trash during a foray through our alley. The Mulhollands, by far the most affluent people on our block, got airmail letters from New York City, of all places.

But the Air-Post Treasures airmail stamps were special. In particular, a 1926 Charles Lindberg set, showing "The Spirit of St. Louis" plane crossing the Atlantic. I immediately plucked the stamps from the sheet. Not cheap—sixty cents for the set of three–but I had to have them.

A True Crime Story

The zeppelin on the following page was a rare stamp. Issued in 1933 in limited quantities, the fifty-cent airmail was very popular with collectors. I'd seen pictures of it in the library's stamp magazines, but I never thought I'd ever have a chance to own one. There was a 1937 China Clipper set and 1937 six-cent American eagle. I finally had to restrain myself. A dollar and seventy-five cents was enough for one day. I opened up my bank for the money.

There was ninety-five cents left in the bank.

I stared at the coins in disbelief. What happened to all of my money? Only weeks ago there'd been a lot of cash in the savings bank. Could I have possibly spent all of it on stamps?

Looking at the airmails I'd picked off the sheets, I realized I'd have to put some back. But which? I couldn't possible give up the Lindberg set. And I certainly had to buy the zeppelin. There would never be another chance to buy another.

I took the coins to pay for the Lindberg and China Clipper sets and the American eagle and put them in the return envelope along with the remainder of the stamps. Maybe Air Post Treasures wouldn't notice that the zeppelin was missing.

By now I was receiving stamp packets in the mail practically every day. Luckily the postman delivered the mail on our street when I was on the way to school, so I was intercepting the stamp packets before my mother saw them.

Air Post Treasures wasn't at all concerned that I hadn't paid for the zeppelin stamp. They merely included a bill in another packet containing more air-mail stamps on approval. I picked out twenty cents worth of stamps and sent them a dime. I was running a tab.

One blustery winter day when playground recess would have been an endurance event, I took my stamp album to school. During recess I opened it up at my desk, knowing that Imogene Poppingail

43

wouldn't be able to resist coming over to see what new stamps I had.

"Who's that man? she asked.

"Charles Lindberg. He flew across the Atlantic Ocean in that plane, 'The Spirit of St. Louis.'"

"You've got a stamp with a blimp on it."

"It's not a blimp. It's a zeppelin. Made in Germany." I was loving this–telling Imogene something she didn't know.

Other kids began drifting over, looking at the stamps as I turned the pages.

Suddenly Miss Smedberg, our fourth-grade teacher was also looking over my shoulder at the album. This was highly unusual since Miss Smedberg never had the slightest desire to know or even think about what the boys in her classroom might be up to on their own time.

"That's a fine stamp collection you have, Gerald."

"Yes, Miss Smedberg." I began flipping the album pages nervously, trying to keep up with my accelerating pulse. I had a mind-numbing crush on Miss Smedberg.

"Where did you get those airmail stamps?" she wanted to know.

"A company in California sent them to me."

"CALIFORNIA???" several kids exclaimed in unison. To anyone living in the U.P., California was a far off magical wonderland where it never snowed, and movie stars drove around in convertibles.

Miss Smedberg treated me to one of her dazzling smiles. "Gerald, perhaps we could put on a special show-and-tell, and you could tell the whole class about your stamps."

"Yes, Miss Smedberg."

ಸಿಂಜ಼

I had to get more stamps. There were still too many countries that I had no stamps for. Too many blank pages in my album for a decent show-and-tell.

A True Crime Story

If Air Post Treasures didn't mind that I ran up a tab maybe the other stamp companies would do the same. From then on whenever I received an envelope full of approval stamps I removed the stamps I wanted and sent back the rest. No money changed hands, the simple reason being that I had no money.

And it worked. The stamp companies kept sending me packets of stamps and included a bill for past transactions. My collection grew by leaps and bounds.

The postman was getting suspicious when I stopped him every day on Second Street to get my mail, but I explained that I was really anxious to see the stamps before I got back from school. He seemed satisfied with that.

The word got around school about my stamp collection. Crud Burtucci, a large fifth grader with bad teeth, came up to me on the playground. "I hear you got a stamp with a bare-naked lady on it."

I nodded.

"I wanna see it."

One did not ignore requests made by Crud Burtucci. On Saturday Crud came over to our house with a few of his friends. I took them up to my bedroom and closed the door.

When they left, my mother said, "It's nice that you're getting other boys to take an interest in stamp collecting."

※※

Then one day I received a thin envelope from the Jolly Badger Stamp Company. There were no stamps in it.

Dear Mr. Harju

It has come to our attention that some time has passed since we have received payment for your recent purchases. We are sure that it is merely an oversight on your part. We would be pleased if you could take time from your busy schedule to send a partial payment on the amount listed below. Thank you for your prompt attention.

Very truly yours
The Jolly Badger Stamp Company

It was a rather polite letter, so I figured that since they were a company in a big city like Milwaukee that sooner or later the Jolly Badger Stamp Company would simply forget about the money. I put the letter in the desk in my bedroom.

Over the next two weeks several more letters arrived from other stamp companies also requesting money. I put them in the desk drawer.

The number of approval packets arriving in the mail had slowed to a trickle. But Miss Smedberg had announced a date for my show and tell. I had to continue taking stamps from the approval sheets I was getting if I expected to amass a collection big enough to be worthy of a show-and-tell in front of Miss Smedberg.

Another letter from the Jolly Badger Stamp Company arrived in the mail, not quite as nice as the previous one.

Dear Mr. Harju
We have not received a reply to our previous letter, nor have we received payment on the amount owed. In order to reestablish our cordial business relationship we must insist on a substantial payment on the amount listed below as soon as possible.

Yours truly
The Jolly Badger Stamp Company

Desperate times called for desperate measures. I crossed the railroad tracks to see my pal, Kippy Jacobs.

A True Crime Story

"Hey, you want my Tom Mix cap gun?"

"The revolver with the wood bullets that slip in and out?"

"Yeah."

"Sure, I want it!"

"I'll sell it to ya for a dollar."

Kippy looked at me with astonishment. "A dollar? I thought you were gonna give it to me."

"I need some money."

"An' you come to see me? Where you think I'd get a dollar from?"

I had similar bad luck trying to sell my Tinkertoys, prized steelie marbles, and an almost-new Gilbert chemistry set. I thought I'd surely get some nibbles on my latest issues of the Green Lantern, Batman, and Captain Marvel comic books, but all the South Ishpeming kids were members of a comic-book-trading network, so everyone knew that sooner or later they'd get to read them for free.

ಬಾ

I began loosing my appetite, and a curious rash developed on my chest. When I got the word "currency" in a spelling bee at school my palms immediately got sweaty and I froze up.

I had one last straw to grasp at. My mother was feeding Sunday's leftover chicken, boiled potatoes and carrots into the meat grinder, the prime ingredients for our weekly supply of hash.

"Mom, ya know how busy you get just before Christmas?"

She paused and looked at me questioningly. "So?"

"You got lots of cooking, Christmas cards to send, wrapping presents . . ."

"Christmas is nine months away. What's this all about?"

"I was figuring you could just give me my Christmas present now. Less work for you at Christmas. An' you wouldn't even haft'a wrap it. Money would be fine."

"Forget it. You'll just have to wait until Christmas."

※

Curt letters from stamp companies were now arriving daily, all asking for money. But the letter that chilled my bones was the one from the Jolly Badger Stamp Company.

> *Dear Mr. Harju*
> *We have gotten no response from you to our previous letters. Unless we immediately receive payment in full for the amount owed we will take legal action.*
> *The Jolly Badger Stamp Company*

I crammed it on top of the alarmingly high stack of letters in my desk drawer. *Legal action? What did that mean?* I lurched downstairs and went into the kitchen.

"Mom, what does legal action mean?"

"Legal action? Well, for instance, if someone owes you money and won't pay you can hire a lawyer to help you get it back."

"How does the lawyer do that?"

"He goes to court and explains to the judge why you should get the money. But the person who owes you the money can hire his own lawyer. This lawyer tells the judge why the money doesn't have to be paid, and then the judge decides what happens."

My mother looked at me curiously. "Why did you ask that question?"

"Oh . . . uh . . . just something Miss Smedberg was talking about."

"She's discussing legal action with fourth graders?"

"Uh . . . well . . . only a little bit."

※

A True Crime Story

I was now having great difficulty sleeping, and when I did get to sleep I dreamt of jail. I finally decided to throw myself on the mercy of the Jolly Badger and wrote a letter.

Dear Mr. Badger
My lawyer says that because I'm only in the fourth grade I don't have to pay because I don't have a job that pays me any money.
Yours truly
Jerry Harju

The following Saturday the mailman delivered our mail while I was eating breakfast at the kitchen table. My mother handed me a letter from the Jolly Badger Stamp Company. Without thinking I tore it open at the table.

Dear Jerry
Unless we receive immediate payment we will have to write a letter to your parents and explain to them how much you owe.
The Jolly Badger Stamp Company

My mother looked at my stricken face. "What's wrong?"

I broke down and confessed everything, paying for the stamps with the money in my bank until there was nothing left in the bank, then keeping more stamps without paying.

By now my mother was sitting at the table, her face a foot from mine. "How much do you owe these people?"

"I . . . I think about sixteen dollars," I blubbered.

She clutched the edge of the table with both hands to keep from falling out of her chair. "Sixteen *DOLLARS??*"

I nodded, crouching down in my chair to make a smaller target.

"You're going to send those stamps back, every one that you didn't pay for."

"But my show-and-tell is next week."

"You take the stamps you didn't pay for and send them back right now!"

"I don't have money for stamps," I said.

"What do you mean? That's how you got into this fix."

"No, I mean I don't have money for stamps to put on the envelopes to send them back."

She thought about that for a moment. "I'll take care of that, you just take care of the rest." She got up from the table and shot me a severe look. "Only ten years old and already a crook." She paused and added, "Well, you're not going to be a crook any more."

෩෬

It took several days to figure out which stamps I hadn't paid for and which company they had come from, but I finally got it all sorted out. I packaged up the stamps into several envelopes and mailed them back to their rightful owners. Within two weeks the nasty letters stopped. I did get a letter from Milwaukee. The Jolly Badger was jolly once more, even suggesting that if I wished they would send me more stamps on approval. I didn't reply.

My mother took possession of my savings bank and changed the combination.

෩෬

Surprisingly, the show-and-tell went off extremely well. When I carried my album into the classroom I felt pretty low. After I'd sent so many stamps back to the companies, the album pages looked awfully bare. But I laid out the loose pages on two long tables at the front of the room. After a short, faltering introduction I told the class to come up and look over the stamps.

Every kid in the class immediately rushed up to the tables, boys and girls alike elbowing for position. Miss Smedberg couldn't get close enough to see the stamps herself, but she was very pleased with the class response and told me later that it was the best show-and-tell she'd ever had.

It might very well have been keen interest in stamp collecting on the part of the fourth graders, but the fact that Crud Bertoucci had passed the word around the school that I had a stamp with a bare-naked lady on it could have contributed to the enthusiasm, I didn't know for sure.

ဢ)ᏣR

Two weeks later I intercepted Imogene Poppingail on the playground during recess to show her my latest stamp acquisition.

"Did you buy these?" she asked.

"No. I don't buy stamps anymore."

"Where did you get them?"

"My grandma sent them to me. They're from Finland. See the 'Suomi' on the stamps? That's Finn for 'Finland'" My mother had recently told her mother in Republic that I was collecting stamps, so my grandmother sent me a bundle of Finnish stamps that she'd gotten from the old country years before.

Imogene looked at the stamps closely. "There's no cancel on these stamps. They haven't been used."

"Yeah. They're called mint stamps. You want some?"

Imogene stared at me. "You'd give me some of these?"

"I got lots of extras."

"Well, sure. That'd be great!"

I began sorting out the duplicate stamps for her. "But you mustn't use hinges on these."

"No hinges? What do you mean?"

"Hinges mess up the gum on mint stamps. You hinge them and they won't be worth as much anymore." I was acquiring a lot of stamp-collecting knowledge from the library copies of *Linn's Weekly Stamp News*.

"How do I put them in my album?" Imogene wanted to know.

"You put them in little cellophane envelopes. I've got some of those that you can have."

Imogene was totally confused by all of this new information. I realized that I would have to sit her down and educate her on the fine art of stamp collecting.

FOOD WE NEVER ATE

When I was a kid, December was the season for eating foods I didn't get the rest of the year. Fruit cakes have always been the butt of jokes, but my mother baked a truly mean one. If she'd had the wherewithal to mass produce and sell her fruit cakes, we'd have been living high on the hog in New York City instead of a drafty wooden house in Ishpeming. We always had Christmas saffron bread, in fact, Mom was still baking it well into her late eighties. Believe it or not, Christmas was the only time of year when we had oranges and nuts.

But many of today's more commonplace foods we didn't eat *ANY* time of year simply because they never found their way up to the U.P. We didn't even know many of them existed.

There wasn't a single Mexican restaurant in the U.P. back then. The only thing I knew about Mexico was that Gene Autry would wander down there occasionally and sing about it, but I never saw him eat anything while he was there.

I was introduced to Mexican food at the age of 19 when I was a University of Michigan co-op student at White Sands Proving Ground, New Mexico. The nearest town was Las Cruces, and one Saturday Bob Kovacs, a fellow Michigan co-oper, and I wandered into a restaurant.

Looking at the menu I said, "What is this stuff? What's an en-chee-la-daw?"

"Enchilada. It's Mexican food," Bob replied. He was from downstate Owosso and much more cosmopolitan than I was.

I ordered enchiladas, and after the first forkful I was hooked. Every Saturday thereafter Bob and I would ride the Army bus the 28 miles to Las Cruces for Mexican food. Kovacs finally got tired of it, and from then on I made the journey alone.

When I was a kid our seafood consisted of what was caught in the local lakes and streams plus canned sardines and the occasional tin of kippered herring. During World War II we moved to Milwaukee and one day went into the Holloway House Cafeteria on Wisconsin Avenue. Sliding my tray past the vast selections of food I pointed at something that resembled skinned caterpillars. "What's that?" I asked.

"Those are shrimp," my mother said. She was very knowledgeable about different kinds of food, being an avid reader of *Woman's Day* magazine.

"What do they taste like?" I asked.

"I don't know," my mother admitted. She had only seen the magazine photos.

My father pointed at a little sign stuck in the shrimp. "An' at that price we ain't gonna find out what they taste like either!"

In the early 60's I was between wives and living in Santa Monica, California. One night I decided to go out and eat Italian, mainly because I couldn't afford steak. At that time my only exposure to Italian food had been spaghetti and meatballs, but I'd heard about pizza and that night decided to give it a try.

"What would you like on your pizza?" the waitress asked.

"What are the choices?"

"We have a lot of different things. You can have anything you want on it."

"Well, give me the works."

Her eyebrows shot up. "Everything?"

"Everything."

"What size would you like?"

"Well, I'm pretty hungry. Make it a large."

Her voice lowered respectfully. "One large with the works, coming up."

What arrived at the table was the size of a manhole cover, only heavier. The steaming pizza was topped with pepperoni, anchovies, three different kinds of Italian sausage, black olives, green pepper, six varieties of mushrooms, garlic, broccoli, bacon, chicken, minced onions, sliced tomatoes, spinach, pineapple chunks, and 16 different cheeses. Diners at nearby tables twitched their noses, turning to see where the bizarre aroma was coming from.

I had been brought up to finish all the food on my plate, but after the fifth slice my eyeballs rolled back in my head, and I had to call it a day. I've never had much use for pizza since.

There were also no Chinese restaurants in the U.P. My mother made something involving leftover beef and white rice that she called chop suey, but I found out later that it wasn't even close. I still don't know what Peking duck tastes like. I don't know when bagels arrived in the U.P., but it was well after I'd left for college.

There were a lot of foods that I had my fill of when I was a kid–oatmeal, hash, mojakka, boiled carrots, jello, rice pudding, and rhubarb. If you ever invite me to dinner and any of those items are on the menu, let me know, I'll make sure to bring plenty of wine to wash it down with.

෨○ඎ

KIDS GOING TO WAR

By June, 1942 our country had been engaged in World War II for six months. The shock of the Pearl Harbor attack had worn off, and the whole nation was gearing up for a conflict the likes of which the world had never seen. Every American was involved. Millions of young men and women were joining the Army, Navy, Marines, and Coast Guard. Ford, General Motors, and Chrysler were feverishly converting over auto assembly lines to build planes and tanks. Housewives were learning how to rivet and weld on these assembly lines to replace the men going into the service. Oldsters willingly stepped out of retirement to be trained as air raid wardens and submarine spotters.

And kids did their part. Every Friday we lined up at school, clutching our dimes and quarters to buy defense stamps from our home room teacher. Before the war boys were never found in gardens; that was only for mothers, girls, and sissies. But the snow had no sooner melted when I was dribbling carrot and radish seeds into the dirt in our backyard for my first Victory Garden. My bedroom walls were papered with silhouettes of enemy warplanes so I could make a ready identification should a squadron of German Heinkel 111's make a surprise bombing attack on Ishpeming. Those were exciting times.

But things changed. When school let out my defense-stamp

connection disappeared. The Victory Garden was coming up nicely, only needing an occasional watering. Every German and Japanese warplane silhouette on my walls was committed to memory. Summer vacation had arrived–I always loved it–but now it was different. Everyone was totally absorbed in the war effort except me. I suddenly found myself without a way to show my patriotism.

Other kids felt the same. We went through the motions of the usual summertime activities, but our hearts weren't in it. No one cared who won or lost the "keepsies" marbles games, which in years past had been a blood sport. We taped up our baseball and bats and played street ball, but it was a listless effort at best.

Then one day my mother said there was a piece in the *Mining Journal* that might interest me. It seemed that President Roosevelt was declaring that the boys and girls of America could perform a great patriotic service for their country by helping the National Salvage effort, that is collecting scrap metal, rubber, rags and paper.

If there was anything close to the hearts of Ishpeming kids, it was collecting trash. Every day we religiously scoured the alleys looking for any "good stuff" to take home. Now we were true patriots.

The rules were simple. We would collect piles of scrap metal, rags, paper, and rubber, and when notified, the city would come around and pick up the piles. Our gang quickly spread out over every alley in south Ishpeming. We snatched up all the old *Mining Journals* and *Reflectors* and brushed away the flies to dive into garbage cans for empty vegetable, soup, and beer cans. Tinfoil from empty cigarette and chewing-gum packages was laboriously peeled off and formed into large balls.

We inspected miles of LS&I ore-train tracks where we found stray railroad spikes laying on the railway bed. So many spikes wound up in our scrap-iron pile that the Ishpeming city fathers got concerned that kids were prying them loose from the rails. We would never have done anything like that, though.

Kids Going to War

Rags were a different proposition, hard to find because a Great Depression hangover kept people darning their socks and shirts and sewing up holes in bed sheets. But we grabbed up every filthy, oily rag we could find.

There wasn't a whole lot of scrap rubber either. Motorists were driving on tires that you could practically see through because new ones were impossible to get during the war. Later on the tire situation got even tougher. The government enacted the Idle Tire Purchase Plan which in effect dictated that civilian car owners were only allowed to possess the four mounted tires and one spare for their car. Any tires in excess of that had to be sold or given away to a scrap dealer. Stories circulated around that motorists who were foolish enough to carry two spares on their car soon found that parties unknown had relieved them of the extra spare tire. We kids would never have done anything like that, though.

Salvage collection was soon a juvenile obsession all over Ishpeming. It became a sporting frenzy where groups of kids scouted out salvage piles all over town to see who had the biggest haul. One day we sauntered over into the territory of our arch enemy, the Catholic kids, to take a look at their scrap-iron pile. Furious at the intrusion, they hurled railroad spikes at us to drive us away. We scooped up the spikes and took off to add them to our pile.

Adults began taking unusual precautions for fear that everything would now be considered prime salvage material. People chained their lawnmowers to trees and then realized that the chain might be taken, too. Women kept a watchful eye on their good nylon stockings drying on the clothesline thinking that a kid might come along and realize that nylons were good parachute material. We kids would never done anything like that, though.

By the time school started again in September we had picked the town clean. In three months Ishpeming had gotten a glorious face lift. Junked cars no longer lounged around in empty weed-covered lots.

You couldn't find a single loose railroad spike near the LS&I tracks. Old newspapers or tin cans weren't in the alleys because they were now being packaged up by folks turning them in themselves. It was time to go back to buying defense stamps.

On the first day of school a story was going around that one of the teachers was very upset because that morning she came out to find someone had removed the steel front bumper from her Model A Ford.

We kids would never have done anything like that, though.

A TIME FOR MODEL BUILDING

The month of February was always the transition between winter and spring. By then we'd been frolicking in the snow for two or three months, and you can peg just so many snowballs at the Catholic kids and make just so many snow forts and take just so many headers while ski jumping before it all got pretty tame. March was still weeks away when we would begin pawing around in the dirty slush with soaked mittens looking for a patch of bare ground so we could start playing marbles. In March we also became busy in neighborhood woodsheds, winding fresh tape around cracked bats in anticipation of street baseball. But March was in the distant future, so every February I rekindled the passion for my favorite indoor pastime–building model airplanes.

These days if a kid wanders into the toy department in Wal-Mart, looking for model airplanes, what he'll find are, in fact, perfect miniature airplanes–no assembly required. The only challenge is trying to weasel $40 out of his mother so he can buy one.

A 1940's model airplane kit was a different story–a *LOT* of assembly required. The kit consisted of a cardboard box filled with sheets of balsa wood, pieces of white tissue paper, and a large sheet of instructions with a 3-D illustration of the model-airplane skeleton. Zillions of structural components were all labeled with their own unique number, to be placed in the exact proper location in the model. The kit typically cost 25 cents but required $10,000 (1940 dollars) in labor costs to put the $#@!! thing together.

The tiny balsa-wood parts, when put together, resembled the airframe of a real plane. The parts were printed on thin balsa sheets, and the initial task was to carefully cut them out with a sharp razor blade. This took a *LONG, LONG* time, and the parts were often soaked with blood from the unfortunate model builder if he had an off day with the razor blade. This was long before the Consumer Products Safety Commission began watchdogging toy manufacturers.

These pieces became formers on the fuselage and ribs on the wings and tail surfaces: cross-sectional slices of the airplane joined together with long, thin balsa rods called stringers to form the model skeleton.

Everything was bonded together using model-airplane cement, a transparent adhesive that quickly hardened into a rocklike consistency. Nothing would dissolve it. To get it off your fingertips you had to take the skin with it. Mothers of model-airplane enthusiasts quickly learned to make sure her kid was dressed in well-worn clothes when he was working on the model because the only way to get airplane cement from clothing was with scissors. The precise, exacting work of model building wasn't made any easier by the fact that the fumes from the model-airplane cement had a tendency to severely erode motor skills. But if you inadvertently inhaled too much of it you didn't really care.

Next came the "engine." The kit contained a long rubber band which was stretched from a wire hook in the tail assembly through the airframe to the propeller fixed on the front cowl. Turning the propeller many times with your finger twisted the rubber band. When released, the prop would spin rapidly for a few moments, providing thrust for flight. Actually, it almost never worked, and after spending countless hours putting the model together no one ever took the chance trying to make it fly.

The skin for the airplane was white tissue paper. This operation was even more dicey than cutting out airframe pieces with the razor blade. Segments of tissue paper were carefully laid on the model and fastened in place with several tiny drops of airplane cement. Taking your mother's sprinkling bottle used to dampen clothes before ironing, you very delicately sprinkled droplets of water all over the tissue paper. This tightened and smoothed the paper, making it much like real airplane skin. The problem was that it frequently didn't work. Too much water in one spot and a hole formed. If one section tightened more than its neighbor, the tissue paper ripped. I finally resorted to using our bug sprayer, throwing out a fine mist of water which worked much better.

But it still looked like tissue paper so next I brushed on a coat of Testors model-airplane dope, paint that binds nicely with paper or cloth. Don't ask me why they call it dope, I don't know. It came in a variety of colors, and you picked out one that matched the real airplane (e.g. blue for a Navy fighter). Testors dope had an even more obnoxious odor than the cement, and by now my mother was good and tired of the toxic fumes drifting downstairs into the kitchen. Every February she loudly suggested that I take up my model building during the summer in the woodshed.

Now came the most fun of all, the final steps of adding realistic touches. The kit contained a clear plastic cockpit canopy, a sheet of decals with colorful wing and fuselage insignias, and tiny machine-gun barrels that went on the leading edge of each wing.

When I finally finished a model I attached a stout thread and hung it from my bedroom ceiling, already dreaming of the next kit I would build. At one time the models hanging in my bedroom were so thick that you couldn't see the ceiling.

I became an expert model-airplane builder. With a double-edge razor blade in my rock-steady fingers, I could perfectly extricate the tiniest, most complex piece from a balsa sheet. I could place two molecules of airplane cement on the end of a stringer and deftly insert it into a small slot on a rib. At the risk of sounding immodest, at age ten I had the hands of a brain surgeon.

    Which is why I was amazed recently when at my cousin Karen's house I assembled a shelf unit that wound up looking like it was drunk. Some skills don't improve with age.

A POSITION OF AUTHORITY

He was about my age–ten or eleven, maybe twelve at the most, so you didn't have to be very old to do what he was doing. He probably went to Kilbourn, but I couldn't know for sure because it was my first day at Kilbourn Grade School in Milwaukee.

He stood on the curb at Wells and 18th St. His dark blue jacket and pants provided good contrast for the gleaming white Sam Browne belt with the silver badge on the shoulder strap, telling the world that he was responsible for directing traffic.

It was February, 1944, yet he was bare-headed, not a hair out of place in the bitterly cold wind whistling off of Lake Michigan. The kid was my height, but he somehow looked taller.

I pulled up on the sidewalk behind him. He raised his right hand indicating that I needed to stop while cars passed through the intersection. At a moment deemed appropriate, he strode into the middle of the crosswalk, blew the whistle that hung around his neck, and again raised his hand, this time stopping car traffic including a Wells streetcar. With the other hand he motioned for me to cross the street.

The safety cadet eyed me curiously as I stomped into the crosswalk in my oversized Arctic boots and large mackinaw coat.

Northern Tales No. 5

World War II had just provided my parents with good-paying jobs in Milwaukee, but old habits die hard. My mother was still buying my clothes three sizes too large to save money.

Only days ago we'd arrived from Ishpeming, a hardscrabble little mining town in Upper Michigan. No one there had ever heard of safety cadets. Ishpeming's Central Grade School had a tough curriculum, but you were on your own getting back and forth from home to school.

Two school girls–both pretty cute–entered the crosswalk with me, but they didn't even know I was there. Their eyes were fixed on the safety cadet. He gave the girls a deadpan look, but then one eyelid flickered, a shadow of a wink. The girls giggled and then looked away.

I wanted to have that job. I mean, I *REALLY* wanted to have that job.

❧☙

During the next two weeks there was little time to think about becoming a safety cadet. Starting at a new school took a lot of effort. Ishpeming's Central School had equipped me with excellent reading, writing, and arithmetic skills, but getting in step with new textbooks and assignments required time. Fitting into the school's social structure was a bigger challenge. Coming from Upper Michigan, a foreign country, I got the intense "new kid" treatment on the playground by the fifth-grade boys. But since I wasn't the confrontational type, I fit in rapidly. In fact, I received the honor of being invited to join the Gremlins, the Kilbourn Grade School fifth-grade gang.

The gang got their name from a World War II phenomenon when British RAF pilots began reporting sightings of small demons riding both in and outside of their aircraft during missions. These so-called "gremlins" were apparently mechanically inclined since they were supposedly responsible for various aircraft malfunctions, or so the pilots claimed. At first it was thought that gremlins were

A Position of Authority

Nazi sympathizers, but when German pilots also began seeing the creatures on the wings of their Messerschmitts, pulling off pla[nty of] little pranks like loosening the ailerons, it was concluded tha[t the] gremlins weren't taking sides in the conflict.

Unlike the wartime gremlins, the Kilbourn School Gre[mlins] had no clear cut mission, but it wasn't for lack of trying. Durin[g our] meetings on the school playground we discussed complex m[atters] such as our plans for future sexual encounters with girls and [the] resistance to mount should German paratroopers land in Milw[aukee].

At one Gremlin meeting I brought up the issue of becoming a school safety cadet.

Murph, the chief Gremlin, scowled at me, "Whaddaya wanna be a safety cadet for?" Joining organizations that involved wearing regulation gear like a Sam Browne belt and a badge was counter to Gremlin thinking since we were more a guerrilla group.

Knowing this, I countered quickly. "Being a safety cadet is a good way to pick up girls."

Murph nodded. "Yah, you got sumethin' there." Murph had been selected as the head Gremlin mainly because his theories about girls and sex were more believable than those posed by the rest of the members. "The cadets are picked by Henshaw, the principal. Don't hold your breath, though."

※※※

The following day during recess I timidly knocked on the outer office door of Roland Henshaw, the Principal of Kilbourn Grade School. The principal's secretary let me in and pointed to a chair next to her desk. Moments later I was ushered into the inner office.

Mr. Henshaw was a slight, balding, middle-age man with a small mustache. As we entered, his secretary handed him a file containing my performance record. He glanced briefly at the file and looked up at me.

"Well, Gerald, you seem to be adjusting well to a new school. Now, what can I do for you?"

"Sir, I'd like to be a safety cadet."

Henshaw smiled and nodded. "Yes, and with your grades you're certainly qualified. Unfortunately, right now there aren't any openings. I'm sorry."

Henshaw escorted me to the door, a hand on my shoulder, "Gerald, I hope you continue to do good work in your classes."

"Yes, sir."

༄༅

Weeks later, one Monday morning before classes began, Miss Hobson, our fifth-grade teacher, approached me in the cloak room. "Gerald, Mr. Henshaw would like to see you."

I gulped and my throat tightened. A command to see the school principal was never good news. I reluctantly went downstairs to Henshaw's office.

The principal motioned me to a seat in front of his desk. "Gerald, are you still interested in becoming a safety cadet?"

"Yes, sir!"

He gave me a tight smile. "Well, an opening has suddenly come up."

"Oh? Someone quit?"

"Uh . . . well . . .no, not exactly. Gregory Schultz won't be in school for awhile."

Schultz was a sixth-grader, one year ahead of me, but I knew him from his crosswalk-control post at one of the intersections on my route home. "Uh huh. Is he sick?"

"Uh . . . well . . . he got struck by a bus."

Then Henshaw quickly added, "But he's okay now, just a broken leg and some bruises. He should be back in school in a month or so. You'd be taking over his safety cadet job if you want it.

Struck by a bus. "Uh . . . sure I do."

Henshaw nodded. "Gregory's accident is a stark reminder that you cadets have to be extra careful when you're out on the street. Don't forget that."

I nodded.

The principal said, "Good. After your last class this afternoon go down and see Mr. Phelps in the gym. He'll give you an orientation and the equipment you'll need. You start tomorrow morning."

છાભ

Mr. Phelps was a muscular ramrod-straight person who taught phys-ed to the fifth and sixth-grade boys. He was also responsible for orienting the safety-cadets. I sat on a wooden folding chair as Phelps explained with words and hand motions what I should and should not be doing at the intersection crosswalk. He then handed me a booklet to read, a form for my parents to sign, and a Sam Browne belt, whistle and badge.

I got up to leave when Phelps said, "You know what happened to Schultz, don't you?"

"He got hit by a bus."

"Yeah, but you know why? He was trying to impress a couple of girls from our school who were standing on the curb, so he tried his hand at bullfighting."

"Bullfighting?"

"Well, to be more accurate, busfighting. He went out and stood in the middle of the crosswalk on 18th and Wisconsin waving on the traffic in both directions to see how close the Wisconsin Avenue bus would come to missing him. The girls would love it, he thought. Busfighting. You *NEVER, NEVER* do that, understand? A bull's got two horns, and a bus has only one, but it outweighs a bull by several tons. Go home and read your booklet, and remember what I said."

Northern Tales No. 5

※

My mother looked at the form I handed her. "You want to be a safety cadet? What's that?"

"You direct traffic at the corners so the kids can cross the street on their way to school."

"They want *YOU* to direct traffic?"

"Other boys at school do it. They're my age. It's safe. You gotta whistle around your neck that you blow to stop the cars."

She pursed her lips. "I don't want you doing that. You'll get run over."

"Ma . . . a, I wanna do it. Mr. Henshaw, the school principal, said I'd be good at it."

"He doesn't know you like I know you." She picked up the white Sam Browne belt and looked at it. "What's that stain? It looks like blood."

I hadn't told her about Gregory Schultz. "Probably just dirt."

She looked more closely at the belt. "It doesn't look like dirt. It looks like blood."

"Probably the last kid had a nosebleed. Ma, please sign the form. They want me to start in the morning."

※

Two little boys walked up to the curbside and looked at me expectantly. I held up my hand indicating that they should stop, put the whistle in my mouth and blew it.

One boy looked at the other and sneered. "What a moron!" Then he turned to me. "You don't blow the whistle at us. You blow it at the cars to stop them! What a moron!"

My face got red. I'd only been at the intersection for two minutes, and they were the first kids to arrive, and I had messed up already.

A Position of Authority

I looked at the morning traffic on Wisconsin Avenue, which was pretty heavy. The safety cadet instructions were clear. A cadet waited for a letup in the traffic before he walked into the crosswalk, held up his hand to stop the vehicles, and blew his whistle. But a heavy volume of cars and trucks kept whizzing by. I waited.

One of the little boys snapped at me. "Well, whaddaya waiting for? My geography class starts in twenty minutes!"

The other one piped up. "I think he's waiting until school is out for the year so he can just go home for summer vacation."

Smart alecs. Just then the traffic lightened up. I walked into the crosswalk, held up my hand to stop the oncoming cars and blew the whistle. They slowed to a halt.

It worked. *I could actually stop traffic.*

But my exhilaration was short lived. Moments later Clyde (a.k.a. Boo) Hicks arrived at the intersection. Hicks was a pudgy sixth grader with a disposition as ugly as his crooked teeth. His favorite trick was to come up behind a lower grade boy, grab the seat of his pants and violently jerk upward, standing the boy on his tiptoes, then yelling "Boo!" So everyone called him Boo but not to his face.

As Boo got to the curb I put up my hand motioning for him to stop. Boo slapped the hand aside and strode into the crosswalk. Cars screeched to a halt, horns blaring. Unconcerned, Boo kept moving across the street.

The same thing happened in the afternoon when school let out. The traffic was particularly heavy, but again Boo just stepped off the curb and began to cross the street, holding up his hand to stop the traffic. A woody station wagon bearing down on the intersection at good speed screeched to a halt. The driver stuck his head out the window and yelled obscenities at the fat kid.

I darted into the crosswalk and blew my whistle to stop the cars so they wouldn't hit him. Boo sneered and told me to get back on the curb where I belonged.

And of course it occurred again the next morning. The thought crossed my mind to report Boo to the school principal, but for sure I'd be branded as a rat fink, a reputation no fifth grader needed. Additionally, Henshaw would immediately conclude that I couldn't handle the safety cadet job.

That afternoon at recess the Gremlins clustered in a tight defensive knot for protection against the chilly March wind scudding across the playground. I brought up the issue of Boo Hicks.

Murph said, "Y'mean he just walks out into the street before you tell him he kin go?"

I nodded.

One of the other Gremlins piped up. "Somebody ought'a teach Boo a lesson."

Murph's eyes lit up and a nasty grin crept across his freckled face. The Gremlins finally had a mission.

※

When school let out that afternoon Boo Hicks arrived at my intersection as usual. This time he was going to have a bigger audience for his derring-do feat because I was holding back a group of smaller children waiting for the traffic to let up. Boo pushed the kids aside and marched into the crosswalk to a chorus of blaring horns and screeching brakes. But his smirk faded when he spotted four Gremlins waiting for him on the opposite curb.

"Hi, Boo," Murph said, "We see yer doing yer best to get hit by a bus."

Melvin Jarowski, the biggest Gremlin who we called "Hippo," joined in. "His best ain't so good. He's still standing."

"Maybe we should help Boo out," Murph added.

Boo reached the curb where the Gremlins were blocking his path. "Get outta my way."

A Position of Authority

Murph and Hippo each grabbed one of Boo's arms. "We're gonna give ya some tips on how to get hit by a bus," Murph said. "It'll only take a minute."

Boo thrashed around, trying to free his arms when the other two Gremlins each grabbed a leg and hoisted him in the air. The four gang members, each holding onto a limb, had Boo in a horizontal position a foot off the sidewalk. They began swinging him back and forth in an arc.

The traffic was still heavy, and my group of small kids and I were watching from the opposite curb. The kids screamed in anticipation of seeing something bad about to happen to Boo Hicks.

"Here comes a bus now," Murph cried. "On the count of three we toss him!" Standing at the edge of the curb the four began swinging Boo in a higher arc.

"One!" Murph cried.

Only then did Boo realize what the Gremlins were intending to do. He began yelling bloody murder.

A large trolley bus was quickly bearing down on them, fat sparks of electricity snapping on the ends of the two trolley poles as they crossed junctions of the overhead wires.

"Two!" The Gremlins swung Boo even higher, his ample behind now extending out over the street gutter.

"No! Stop! Stop!" Boo screamed. "Uncle! Uncle!"

"Three!" Murph yelled. But rather than slinging Boo out into the path of the bus the four gang members unceremoniously dropped him butt first onto the sidewalk.

The kids on my side of the street clapped and cheered, but I could see that a few were disappointed that the Gremlins hadn't thrown him out in the street under the bus.

While Boo lay in a quivering heap on the sidewalk, Murph leaned over and advised him that in the future it would be good if he obeyed the safety cadet at the curb.

After that the safety cadet job went very smoothly. I hadn't engineered the radical move that Murph pulled on Boo Hicks; that was his own idea, but it sure worked. After that Boo never gave me any trouble at the intersection. In fact, I never saw him again before or after school. He must have crossed the street in the middle of the block somewhere.

The school kids began treating me with a great deal of respect, mainly because what the Gremlins did to Boo quickly spread around school. The word was out that I had connections.

Then one Friday in April Miss Hobson approached me again in the cloakroom before classes and said, "Mr. Henshaw would like to see you."

Ohmygawd, I thought. Greg Schultz is back in school, and I'll have to give him back the safety-cadet job. With a heavy heart I trudged down to the first-floor office.

Mr. Henshaw greeted me with a bright smile. "Good morning, Gerald. I hear that you're doing well in your classes and also as a safety cadet."

"Thank you, sir," waiting for the axe to fall.

Henshaw glanced down at a list on his desk. "Gerald, beginning on Monday would you assume the position of captain of the safety cadets?"

I didn't hear that right. For a minute I thought he asked me to be captain of the safety cadets. "Sir, what was that you just said?"

"I said, would you take the job of captain of the safety cadets starting this Monday?"

"But . . . sir, I'm only in the fifth grade." I immediately regretted saying that. Maybe he thinks I'm in the sixth.

Henshaw smiled. "I know. Safety cadets are usually sixth-grade boys. We made you the exception because of the sudden opening,

A Position of Authority

and the fact that you're an outstanding student. But the position of captain rotates every two weeks among all of the cadets. Gregory Schultz's turn comes up this Monday, and since you took his place it's your turn. Do you want to do it?"

"Oh, yes sir! I do!"

※

Mr. Phelps handed me a map. "I've marked the intersections where all of the safety cadets are stationed in the morning and afternoon. The captain's job is to make the rounds and handle any problems the boys might have." Then with a sly look, "I hear you're real good at handling problems, eh?"

"What problems, sir?"

"Boo Hicks gave all the cadets a rough time but not anymore."

"Oh, I had nothing to do with that, Mr. Phelps. Some guys I know . . . "

"Yeah, yeah, I understand. But if any of the cadets have problems with rowdy kids at the crossings, not obeying the rules, maybe your friends . . . you know what I mean. . . But don't tell Mr. Henshaw I said that."

"Oh, no Mr. Phelps."

He handed me a Sam Browne belt. "Here's the captain's belt to wear when you start on Monday."

The captain's belt was white, like the one I'd been wearing, but it had twin blue pinstripes running along all of the edges, designating, of course, the higher rank. But the badge fastened to the belt was truly a thing of beauty.

The badge was in the shape of a shield enclosed in a wonderful new material called plastic. At the top of the shield arcing over the Milwaukee city seal were "THE CITY OF MILWAUKEE SCHOOL SYSTEM." On the bottom in larger letters was SAFETY CADET.

Right in the center on top of the city seal in splendid gold block letters was "CAPTAIN."

I took the belt and badge and hurried home.

❧☙

"Ma, look at this."

My mother was in the tiny kitchen of our apartment making meatballs from leftovers. "What . . . it's your safety cadet belt."

"No, look close at it."

She stared at the white belt and badge. "Captain?"

"Starting on Monday I'm captain of all of the safety cadets at Kilbourn School."

No congratulations, just a question. "How come you're captain? We haven't been here that long."

"Everybody gets a turn at it. Mine starts on Monday. Can we go down to Gimbels tomorrow and buy me a blue sweater?"

My mother looked at me curiously. I had never asked for new clothes. "You don't need a new sweater. You've got two nice plaid sweaters that I just bought for you."

"I need one in one color–blue–so the cadet belt stands out better."

She put the meatballs in the oven. "You're not going to be running around outside in just a sweater. It's not that warm yet. You'll have that belt on over your coat. Go wash up for supper."

❧☙

Sunday night we were gathered around our huge Zenith radio listening to Jack Benny when my throat began feeling scratchy. I was making funny grating noises when my mother asked what was wrong.

"Oh, my throat feels a little funny."

She got up from her chair, came over and told me to open wide. "Hmm, it looks pretty red." She placed her hand on my forehead. "You're a little hot, too. You might be coming down with something."

The sheer magnitude of what she had just said hit me. I couldn't be getting sick! I was going to be captain of the safety cadets tomorrow morning! "Ma, I'm okay. My throat's feeling better already!"

She shook her head. When my mother decided that I was sick, then, by God, I was sick, and nobody was going to talk her out of it. "Get ready for bed. I'll fix something for that throat."

In our small Milwaukee apartment I slept on a Murphy bed in the living room that pulled down from the wall. My father pulled the bed down while I got into my pajamas. Mom was busy in the kitchen, and after I'd climbed into bed she brought out a steaming cup of some strange brew.

"Here, drink this down."

My big mistake was not sniffing the cup's contents before taking a big swallow. It burned like a hot poker being shoved down my throat.

"Ghaaaaaaahhhhh . . . . WHAT.... IS....THAT?"

She said, "Don't be a baby now, it's just a spoonful of Sloan's Liniment in warm water. Good for the throat."

Sloan's Liniment was originally developed for relieving muscle fatigue in draft horses. Before long it was found to be beneficial for the same problem in humans, but was never meant for internal consumption. However, that didn't phase my mother. She was convinced that a doctor's care was expensive and unnecessary, and she swore by a legion of home remedies good for whatever afflicted the human body. All of them were radical departures from anything a physician in his right mind would ever prescribe.

The liniment cure had no apparent effect. An hour later when I opened my mouth to tell my mother how good I was feeling only croaking sounds came out. She shook her head again and went back into the kitchen and came out with another cupful of something.

"No, no," I croaked weakly. "Not again!"

She handed me the cup. "This is different, and you don't drink it. Just gargle."

I definitely had to be well by morning so anything was worth a try. I tentatively took a mouthful and began gargling. Some of it leaked down into my throat.

"ERK . . . ERK . . . ERK . . . WHAT IS THIS?"

"It's just vinegar with salt and pepper. People use it for sore throats."

What people, I thought. Martians? I gargled some more and lay back in bed, beginning to feel really bad. My father was sitting next to the radio, listening to Gabriel Heater broadcasting the war news. Heater's doomsday tone was an appropriate background for the way I was feeling.

I was just drifting off to sleep when my mother sat on the edge of the Murphy bed. "Open the top of your pajamas."

"Wha . . . what for?"

She unbuttoned my pajama top and placed something hot, moist and very smelly on my chest.

Laying on my back I stared down at a bundle wrapped in cheesecloth perched on my chest. "Whew, it smells! What is it?"

"A poultice. It'll clear up your chest."

I poked the cheesecloth with a finger. "What's inside of it?"

"Boiled onions."

"BOILED ONIONS?"

"Just lie still on your back and let it do its work. Try to get some sleep."

It's not easy to go to sleep when you're snuggled up to a bag of cooked onions.

ಸಿಧ

A Position of Authority

I suffered through a terrible night, waking up several times, coughing and shivering. Sometime in the early morning hours my mother turned on the light and covered me with another blanket. Then she pushed a spoon toward my mouth. "Open up and swallow."

I swallowed. It was awful. "Cod liver oil?" I squeaked pitifully.

"With ground up aspirin," she said. "Go back to sleep."

Daylight was filtering through the lacy curtains on the living room window when I realized that my face was pressed into the cold, soggy poultice. The whole world smelled like onion.

My mother entered the apartment carrying paper sacks. She said, "I used the phone in the lobby and called in to work and told them I've got to take the day off to take care of you."

I struggled with the bed clothes and sat up. "No you don't. It's Monday and I gotta go to school. It's my first day of being captain of the cadets." I shakily stood up.

With one hand she pushed me back onto the bed, and with the other hand stuck a thermometer in my mouth. "You're not going anywhere. Now shut up and let me take your temperature."

Moments later she looked at the thermometer. "Over 100. Lay back down and cover up."

"Ma, I gotta get going. I can't be late on the first day!"

"Do you know what time it is now? It's ten o' clock. I've already walked over to the school and told them you were sick."

I slumped back on the pillow. "Well, I hope they let me start the captain's job tomorrow. I'll just rest up today and get well."

"From the looks of you, I don't think you'll be in any shape to go to school tomorrow or even Wednesday."

She went over to our small dining table and began to empty the paper sacks she had carried in. I watched as she unloaded an assortment of exotic spices, molasses, garlic, horseradish, several different kinds of tea, and turnips. It was clear that Mom wasn't going to let my illness get the upper hand. She was mounting a vigorous frontal assault with every remedy that she could muster up. All of this stuff was going to go in me. My stomach lurched at the thought.

She pushed another spoonful of cod liver oil into my mouth. As I was gagging she said, "When I went over to the school I took the captain's belt along. Miss Hobson thanked me for bringing it because she said they'll have to give the job to another cadet. She hopes you get well soon."

I crawled well beneath the blankets. This was, without question, the worst day of my life.

Tuesday and Wednesday were no better. Everything ached. I sneezed, blew my nose, and coughed up disgusting blobs. The fever kept me buried under blankets day and night.

The remedies were worse than the illness. I quit asking what I was being given. I didn't want to know. I drank an evil concoction that smelled and tasted like burnt rubber. A gloppy mess put on my chest hardened into a concrete-like shell that clung like a second skin.

Finally Wednesday night my father decided to take matters into his own hands because he was having trouble hearing Gabriel Heater over my coughing and moaning. He left the apartment and returned shortly with a bottle in a paper bag.

A half pint of brandy.

My mother, a card-carrying Lutheran, was aghast. "You can't give him that!"

"Yes I can." The old man broke the seal on the bottle and poured a generous glug into a water glass. "Here, drink it down."

It burned going down my throat, but didn't taste near as bad as what my mother had been serving up.

He poured out another generous amount and handed me the glass. "Down the hatch."

A Position of Authority

This time my eyes watered, and the room began taking on a curious tilt.

"That's enough!" my mother snapped. "He'll get drunk!"

Too late, Ma. I closed my eyes.

ෂ)ෆ

In the morning I woke up in soaked bed clothes. Messy, but amazingly I felt better. Still a bit of a cough, but my head felt much clearer and no chills.

My mother came out of the bedroom and stuck the thermometer in my mouth. She looked at my sodden pajamas and dug out a clean pair, looked down my throat and then at the thermometer. "No fever. Your throat looks okay. You're getting well."

"Do you think it was the brandy?"

She gave me a skeptical look and sniffed. "I doubt it." Lutheran ladies believed that alcohol never solved anything.

"Ma, I'm hungry."

"I can heat up some of that cooked turnip I gave you yesterday."

"How about some Wheaties."

ෂ)ෆ

On Monday I was back at school, physically feeling well but bitterly disappointed at missing my chance at being captain of the safety cadets. While I was sick Greg Schultz, his broken leg out of the cast, returned to school. He still wasn't moving too swift, so at least I was able to return to my regular cadet duties.

I soldiered on through several weeks of school. By early May I was thinking about summer vacation. My grandmother living in Republic in Upper Michigan wrote and extended an invitation for me to stay with her during the summer months. I could get in plenty of fishing and have lots of opportunities for rooting around in the town dump located next to her house. There were tons of good stuff in the dump, and it was all free for the taking. But the biggest draw of all was having a bedroom all to myself, a vast improvement over the lumpy Murphy bed. I wrote back accepting the offer.

Then one Friday out of the blue Miss Hobson took me aside before recess. "Mr. Henshaw would like to see you."

Henshaw gave me his patented stern school-principal stare as I entered his office. "You still want it?"

"Uh . . . want what, sir?"

He held up the safety-cadet captain's belt, the gold center of the badge glowing from the window sunlight. "The last two weeks of school starts Monday. It's yours for those two weeks if you want it."

My hand shot out, grabbling the belt from his grasp.

୫༠ଓଃ

My new dark-blue sweater provided excellent contrast for the white captain's belt. I looked very official as I strode along with my captain's clipboard. The job was easy, only involving walking to check all of the intersections around the school where the cadets were directing traffic. It didn't require stepping out in the crosswalk, blowing your whistle and hoping that the Packard bearing down on you didn't have a deaf, sight-impaired oldster behind the wheel.

Everything was going very well that morning. I checked in with each cadet and made the appropriate mark on the clipboard paper. Going well, that is, until I reached the last intersection.

Boo Hicks was up to his old tricks again.

Tommy Wiley, a husky cadet, was holding one of Boo's sleeves, trying to keep him on the curb.

Boo was bound and determined that he was going to cross whenever he pleased. "Leggo a me, you crud!"

A Position of Authority

"Cadet Wiley, is there a problem?" I inquired in my best captain's voice.

Boo stared at me and immediately jumped back on the curb, shutting his mouth.

Tommy Wiley saw this and said, "Uh . . . I guess not."

"That's good," I said, making the final check mark on my clipboard.

The whole scene was witnessed by a girl from my class waiting to cross. She had raven-black hair, long eyelashes, and a small mouth shaped like a little pink heart.

I gave her a deadpan look and then flickered one eyelid, a shadow of a wink.

She stared at me and then a hint of a smile. Kind of like Hedy Lamar in *White Cargo*.

༄༅

WHEN DUMPS WERE DUMPS

Recently my cousin Karen has been frantically attacking her yard, planting grass, poking flower seeds in the ground, mounting bird and squirrel feeders on poles and I don't know what all. One day she had to take a load of yard trash to the dump, so I went along to help.

They don't call them dumps anymore. Off US-41 there's a road labeled "Household Hazardous Waste Collection Center." Once inside the area there are several signs explicitly directing you where to go to dump your particular type of throwaways. One sign said "Trash Only–No Tires, Batteries, Metal, Cardboard or Household Garbage." Huh? What exactly is left that's classified as "trash?"

We spotted a "Brush" sign, and Karen steered the Escalade over there since we had only branches and leaves. People take these rules very seriously because that sector had nothing in it but dead trees, branches and leaves–not a single scrap of paper, plastic or metal. Karen had several plastic bags filled with leaves so I dumped the leaves and put all of the empty plastic bags back in the vehicle. I was very law-abiding because there were several pairs of eyes watching our every move, the reason being that people don't often see a Cadillac Escalade in a dump.

These days it's become very complicated to throw stuff away, but when I was a kid it wasn't like that. In the summer of 1945 I was 12 years old, living at an exclusive country club outside of Milwaukee where my parents worked. That summer I was avidly into golf, taking off-the-cuff lessons from the crusty old Scottish club pro whose knowledge of the game was only exceeded by his extensive vocabulary of bad words. My mother decided that I needed a more wholesome atmosphere and bought a train ticket for me to spend the remainder of the summer in Republic visiting Mummu Olander, my very wholesome, very Lutheran grandmother.

Mummu lived on the edge of town near the Republic dump. In 1945 recycling was unheard of, so this dump had *EVERYTHING!* People tossed old clothes, tin cans, three-legged chairs, worn-out rugs, kitchen sinks, mattresses, used motor oil, last week's newspapers, car batteries, broken railroad ties, old inner tubes, not to mention the occasional rusting hulk of a '29 Chevrolet. The Red Owl grocery store also contributed, lugging in tons of rotten fruits and vegetables.

For a 12-year-old boy it was heaven. For the remainder of the summer I spent my waking hours in the dump. What could be better than trotting down to the dump every morning and pawing through the new stuff that had been deposited the previous evening. And it was all free! Like a Wal-Mart with everything 100% off. I would often select the very best household items and tote them home for my grandmother. For some reason Mummu didn't think a whole heck of a lot of my gifts.

When you spend ten hours a day prowling around in a garbage dump you take on, shall we say, a certain exotic scent, an essence of very-old tomatoes, used motor oil, moldy rugs, scorched rubber, whiskey, and maybe a dash of dead dog. As usual, I only had to shower on Saturday nights, but Mummu made sure that my clothes, including shoes, got plenty of soap and water every night.

As you might expect, where there's a plentiful supply of over-ripe food there are rats. The Republic-dump rats weren't your ordinary

When Dumps Were Dumps

every-day rats. No, these rats were the size of beavers, only much quicker. Rat killing at the dump was a popular sport. Older kids had single-shot .22's, but I had nothing but my trusty right arm. The rats squeaked with delight as I ineffectively pegged rocks at them.

One day a kid came up to me and said, "Why don'cha use a slingshot?" I stared at him. I'd never used a slingshot in my life. So he showed me how to make one using a forked poplar branch, two strips of inner tube rubber, and a piece of leather tongue from an old shoe. After that Deadeye Harju had the rats running for cover whenever he drew down on them.

But even more exciting than killing rats at the dump was setting fires. The Republic Dump would have quickly overflowed if it hadn't been for the fact that the combustible materials were regularly torched. No adult had to shoulder the responsibility for setting the fires because kids willingly took on the task.

We usually set the dump fires in the afternoon. If someone dumped a large amount of very inflammable material like motor oil or dried paint in cans, we'd use this as a core and amass wood, cardboard, and paper around it. Car batteries were also really good to add to the mix, and if you had a few tires, so much the better. With the proper ingredients we'd have a roaring inferno in no time, punctuated by sharp explosions throwing who knows what into the air and with luck a thick black greasy smoke that, if the wind was blowing right, would blanket the whole town. What could possibly be better than that?

Everybody agrees that in today's world sorting and recycling all of our throwaways is a good thing for the environment. Still, it's too bad that today's kids will never have a chance to dig around in a dump and take home the good stuff, or plug a few rats, or, yes, even set a dump fire or two. It's better than sitting in front of a computer or TV all day and getting fat.

THE SCIENCE OF DOWNHILL SKIING

One afternoon I was driving past Marquette Mountain and glanced over at the skiers zooming down the slopes. Hey, I thought, that looks like fun. Maybe I should give it a try.

"Hold on," my butt cried, "Don't you remember the last time you tried skiing?"

Watching those skiers brought back memories. In the 1970's my mid-life crisis was in full bloom, which had to be the reason why I thought a 40-something guy raised in the U.P. should have no problem with downhill skiing. I'd never tried downhill skiing, and, in fact, I hadn't put on a pair of skis in over 25 years. But being on skis is like riding a bicycle, isn't it? As a young lad I'd been a ski jumper so downhill should be a piece of cake compared to that.

At the time I lived in the Los Angeles area, just a 1 ½ hour drive to excellent ski slopes in the San Bernadino Mountains. One sunny winter morning I drove up to Lake Arrowhead and went into the pro shop to rent the equipment I'd need.

A pro shop employee brought out skis and poles and then had to patiently explain how the ski binders worked because they were far and away more complex than my old inner tube strips. "Do you need ski boots?" the guy asked. Since I'd worn galoshes during my entire ski-jumping career, I nodded. He took my foot measurements and brought out a huge pair of boots resembling instruments of torture from the Spanish Inquisition but made from materials used on reentry rocket nose cones. He helped me put them on and then cinched up thick straps and slammed shut various buckles.

"Ow! Ow! Ow! Take them off!" my toes cried. Then they blacked out from lack of blood.

"Tight is good," he explained. "If the boots are too loose, you can't control the skis. And if you have a bad fall you don't want the boot to come off and have it and the ski travel down to the bottom of the hill without you."

He then suggested that since the equipment was new to me I should join the next beginner's class which was about to start at the top of the "bunny slope."

Once being a seasoned skier I was certain I'd only have to spend a minimal amount of time with the beginners, but I reasoned that I might hear a few useful tips. I clumped outside in the 25-pound boots and clamped on my skis.

The first thing I noticed was that snow had gotten a lot more slippery since I was a kid. But I dug the ski poles into the snow and tottered, slid and lurched over to the chair lift.

I should mention that I'd never been on a chair lift before, which soon became obvious to the skiers in line behind me. I stepped in front of a moving chair, the chair seat smacked me smartly in the butt, knocking me face first into the snow, skis splayed out to both sides. While I thrashed around, making a snow angel wearing skis, chairs carrying skiers zoomed a foot over my head, the skiers yelling, "Watch out! Watch out!" Someone finally dragged me off to one side. I brushed myself off and somehow struggled onto the lift and journeyed to the top of the bunny slope.

The beginner's class consisted of a group of 10-12-year-olds and me. For the next hour the instructor explained the do's and don'ts of downhill skiing–use of the poles, the crouch, executing the Christie,

The Science of Downhill Skiing

etc. The one maneuver I remembered was the self-explanatory snowplow, useful for stopping to avoid sudden death.

The instructor dismissed the class and told us to make a trial run down the hill. The bunny slope was aptly named–a gentle grade with a long stretch of flat area at the bottom to come to a safe stop. The children and I shoved off.

Okay, so I was the last one to reach the bottom, but I only fell once! I knew it would all come back to me. Confident with my newly awakened skill, I went into the lodge for lunch.

Lake Arrowhead had several ski slopes, and after lunch I stood outside the lodge and studied a large map displaying all of the slopes and which chair lift to use for each. One in particular had a catchy name–Misery Run. I decided to try it.

Misery Run wasn't supposed to be the steepest slope, but when I got off the chair lift I was standing on top of the Sears Tower looking down. And unlike the bunny slope, Misery Run was filled with gullies and hillocks (moguls to you ski fanatics.) To make matters worse there were numerous stands of fir trees, strategically placed in harm's way.

I watched skiers–many of them small children–skillfully tearing down the precipitous grade, shouting with glee as they executed picture-perfect turns. It was the moment of truth. I shoved off.

Perhaps I launched myself at a bit too steep an angle because I took off like a Stinger missile. Just before reaching the speed of sound I decided it was time to snowplow. But turning the ski tips inward merely seemed to kick in the afterburners. In desperation I purposefully fell, and after sliding two hundred yards I finally came to a stop.

Digging snow out of my ears I spotted one of my ski poles planted in the snow up the hill where I'd fallen. From my early ski-jumping days I recalled the herringbone, a technique for traversing up the hill while wearing skis. Laboriously working my way back up to the ski pole, I realized it wasn't a wise move. I was going the wrong way in heavy traffic. Skiers were rocketing down the hill, missing me by mere inches and screaming unprintable opinions on what I was doing.

I finally reached my ski pole. As I leaned over to grab it, still facing uphill with my skis in a V position, I began to slip backwards. The next thing I knew I was speeding down the hill again–this time backwards. The skis cried, "Hey, we're not designed for this."

The backs of the skis dug in the snow, and after somersaulting two or three times I smashed up against a spruce tree. Spitting out spruce needles and thankful it wasn't an oak tree, I looked down the hill trying to spot another stand of spruce to aim for.

Ten minutes later I was back down at the lodge. I brushed the snow off and checked for broken bones. I seemed to be okay but my back side argued with that assessment. Of course, a true California skier doesn't shell out big bucks for a lift ticket and then make only one run down the hill. I staggered over to the chair lift and tried it again.

After reminiscing for a moment at Marquette Mountain I kept on going. I headed home and crawled into my recliner with a glass of wine. That's a winter sport I'm really good at.

SENIOR YEAR

I stood in the middle of our living room in my long underwear. My mother was stooped over in front of me with her tape measure and ran it down my inseam. "30 . . . hmmm, I'll make it 31, you're still growing."

"Ma . . . I'm almost eighteen years old and six feet tall. I'm done growing. I don't wanna be swimming around in that suit!"

She straightened up and jotted down a number on the Montgomery Ward order form, then whipped the tape measure around my waist. "Done growing, huh? I've got news for you. You've got a 29-inch waist. You're a bean pole, so you've got a lot of growing to do yet. This suit will cost over twenty dollars, and I'm not going to order one that you'll grow out of in six months. I'll make that a 32-inch waist." She made another entry on the order form.

"Ma, it'll be way too big. I'm going to look . . . rotten in that suit at graduation." I almost said "look like hell," but that kind of language was totally unacceptable in my mother's Lutheran household.

"Don't worry. I'll take in the waist and hem up the legs. You'll look just fine. Now go and get dressed or you'll be late for school. And take the Ward order to the post office on your way." It took me awhile to get bundled up. It was early February and the thermometer outside of our back door read five below zero. Cold weather rarely raised local eyebrows since on any given winter day Upper Michigan often held the dubious distinction of posting the coldest temperature in the 48 states.

My mother handed me the Montgomery Ward envelope as I headed out the door. "Have you talked to Mr. Hooker about your college plans?"

"Not yet. I'm going to meet with him during my study-hall period today."

I may have been almost 18 years old and six feet tall, but I wasn't nearly old enough nor big enough to handle life's decisions. Two weeks prior I had received a cheery congratulatory letter from the University of Michigan informing me that I was the recipient of a state Regents Alumni scholarship paying my college tuition for four years. Good news, right? Wrong. Going to college was not my idea, it was my mother's.

Following graduation from Republic High School I was itching to move to Milwaukee, get a good-paying job as a tool and die maker, buy a new Buick with the exhaust ports in the front fenders and chase women. But my mother flatly stated "It's college or else!" I didn't know what the "or else" was, but I was willing to bet that it didn't involve moving to Milwaukee and chasing women.

Along with the scholarship letter the U. of M. included a form to be filled out indicating which of their colleges I wished to enter. No easy decision for an 18-year-old brain under the influence of raging hormones and dreams of easy money.

I had no idea what to put down as my major. When I was a little kid I loved Tinkertoys, so much so that for three or four years running I found a new set under the Christmas tree. At age ten I had amassed the largest collection of Tinkertoys in the civilized world. I never cared to build the conventional gadgets suggested on the can by the manufacturer. I had to design my own contraptions. So I thought, what the heck, a Tinkertoy genius would make a good engineer. I filled out

Senior Year

the form advising the U. of M. that I wanted to enroll in the College of Engineering. Made good sense to me.

☙❧

My first class was chemistry, but that morning the seniors had a different assignment during first period. We had to select a script for the annual Senior Class Play.

Theodore Hankis, the chemistry teacher, was chairing the discussion. It was apparent that he didn't think much of this job, but the school superintendent, Ichabod Schuyler, had stuck him with it.

On his best day Hankis could be described as surly, and his physical appearance was a perfect match for his disposition–a Hitler mustache, thick neck, broad shoulders and stumpy legs. As a young man Hankis had tried professional wrestling but couldn't make a living at it so he turned to teaching. Everyone called him Tank but not to his face.

Hankis sat at his desk hunched over an open catalog of high-school plays. "Let's see . . . this one takes place in Victorian times. A young lady gives advice to her eager suitor on how to favorably impress her wealthy parents who live in Boston. . . . "

"Nooooo!" cried several senior boys in the back of the room.

"That sounds like a good one," Margaret Koski volunteered.

"It's terrible!' the boys shouted.

Hankis glared over the top of his reading glasses. "Shut up back there! We're going to conduct this in a civilized manner."

He turned another page. "Hmmm . . . this one takes place in a small southern town in the '20's. A young farm hand is on trial for attacking the farm owner's daughter in the barn hayloft. No, I guess not." He turned the page.

"Hey, let's do that one!" Otto Laske blurted out. "I'll be the young farm hand!"

"No!" several girls exclaimed.

"Yeah!" Otto countered.

"Be quiet, Otto!" Hankis snapped. "We're not doing that play, and that's final!"

Several more plays were discussed, but each one was voted down by either the girls or the boys. Hankis was clearly getting fed up with the whole process. He was only at ease issuing ultimatums not practicing democracy.

"Let's go back to the one about sex in the hay," Otto chirped from the back.

Hankis' face turned beet red. He jumped up and bolted to the back of the classroom. His right hand snatched Otto's shirt front, jerking him to his feet. Otto's chair tipped over with a clatter.

"Otto," Hankis hissed. "Do you remember what happened the last time we tangled?"

Otto nodded. He remembered very well. Months earlier while Hankis was writing chemistry reactions on the blackboard, his back to the class, Otto launched a spitball that struck him smartly on the ear.

Hankis spun around and glared at all of the boys, and in a split second singled out the guilty party.

Hankis charged over to Otto and hauled him out the door. The chemistry classroom was on the top floor of the building with the stairwell right outside the door. With one hand grasping the seat of Otto's pants and the other on the back of his belt Hankis tried to throw Otto down the stairs, grunting mightily with each attempted toss. Only by hanging on to the bannister with both hands did Otto save himself.

This time, however, Hankis merely let go of Otto's shirt and returned to his desk at the front of the room and resumed leafing through the play catalog. He abruptly stopped.

"Here's one. This is it. A three-act farce."

Senior Year

"What's a farce?" one of the boys asked.

"It's a comedy," Hankis replied. "It's perfect since this class is full of comedians. The title of this play is 'In Spring the Sap.' Otto, you've been wanting to play the lead so bad. You can be the sap." Hankis treated us to one of his rare chuckles.

☙❧

During my afternoon study-hall period I went down to the principal's office on the first floor. Clarence Hooker, the school principal, was also our senior-class advisor, and he had scheduled the meeting to discuss my college plans. Hooker motioned me to a chair. "Congratulations on the scholarship," he said with a grin. "Have you decided on a major yet?"

I told him about the decision on engineering.

Hooker's smile faded. "Uh huh. Well, that's good, I guess. One problem I'd better tell you about, though."

"What's that?"

"You're math deficient for their engineering entrance requirements."

"Whaddaya mean?"

"We never have enough students choosing the academic curriculum to offer higher level math courses. Out of 29 seniors only six of you are in the academic program. For engineering the U. of M. will expect you to have had solid geometry and college algebra, and you haven't had either of those."

This was not good. "What can I do?" I asked.

Hooker rubbed his chin. "Well, I'm sure the university has those two courses available, but you'd have to take them during your first semester for no credit. Probably slow up your college graduation." He thought for a moment. "But there's another way. Since I'm the high-school math teacher I could teach those two courses to you privately, beginning right now. Would mean a lot of extra work for you, probably even into the summer. It's up to you."

I didn't like either option. "Maybe I should think about getting into some other field that doesn't require all that math."

Hooker said, "Well, yeah, that's another possibility. Engineering doesn't pay all that much, and in almost any other field you'd get a more well-rounded college life."

"Whaddaya mean?"

Hooker grinned. "Ever hear of a woman engineer? There won't be any girls in the engineering classes."

"No girls?" I squeaked. "No girls?"

"That's right."

That did it. There was no way I was going to go through four years of classes with only guys. I'd die. I had to get into something else. But what?

Hooker said, "You've always had a real talent for drawing. Have you ever thought about being an architect?"

I nearly jumped out of the chair. "That's it! I'll get a letter off to the U. of M. and tell them I'm changing my major from engineering to architecture! Thanks, Mr. Hooker!" I hurried out of the office.

After school I sat in the deserted bookkeeping classroom pecking away on one of the ancient Underwood typewriters preparing a letter that would alter my career path. I was ready to do anything to have girls in my classes.

ಸಿಂಧ

One afternoon a few weeks later Tank Hankis came and got me out of the study hall, and he led me into the corridor.

"I just received the scripts for the Senior Class Play. 'In Spring the Sap,' remember?"

"Yeah, Mr. Hankis, I remember." Why was he singling *me* out

Senior Year

to say this?

Hankis produced a script from his coat pocket. "It's a funny play. Jerry, I think you'd be prefect to play the lead."

"Oh, no, Mr. Hankis, not me. I don't have time for that."

Hankis began thumbing through the script. "Mr. Twibbley is an 89-year-old inventor and justice of the peace. We can fix up your face and hair, and you'd be a riot."

"I thought you said that Otto would be good for the lead."

Hankis scoffed. "Otto is still learning to tie his shoes. He'd never be able to memorize the lines in time. That's where you'd be good, Jer, memorizing."

"I can't do it. Right now I'm trying to straighten out my major with the U. of M. I don't have time for a play."

Hankis fixed me with his don't-give-me-a-hard-time stare. "Why don't you take the script home and read it over," he said in his Boris Karloff voice.

I was doomed.

෴

Clarence Hooker herded all of the seniors into an empty classroom. "It's time to send in the order for graduation caps and gowns. I've got to send in sizes right away, so I'm going to take the measurements this period." He put a tape measure on the desk, and using a yardstick made several pencil marks on the doorjamb for height measurements. He began taking the boy's height, chest and head measurements.

Reino Rovaniemi had carried a bathroom scale into the room, and when Hooker finished taking a boy's measurements Reino got him onto the scale.

"Reino, what are you doing that for?" one of the girls asked.

Reino wrote a weight down on a tablet. "It's for the yearbook.

Statistics of our class, weights, measurements, things like that."

Barbara Bandini stepped forward. "If you think you're gonna get me on that %^&*# scale you gotta another think coming!"

Hooker looked up sharply when he heard a girl using salty language, but said nothing when he saw who it was.

No one ever said a word to Barbara Bandini (a.k.a. Bow Wow) when she was in a bad mood, which was most of the time. Bow Bow had earned her nickname in the third grade when she bit off Toivo Kangas' earlobe during a heated dispute in a hopscotch game, and her disposition hadn't improved since. Now, at eighteen, five-foot-eleven and close to 200 lbs., Bow Wow was one of the biggest seniors in the class, boys included.

"Be a sport, Barbara," Reino told her. "It's all in fun. Seniors are supposed to have fun. Maybe you can even do some of your hog-calling at the commencement ceremony."

"There'll be no hog-calling at the commencement ceremony," Hooker declared.

The mention of hog-calling, Bow Wow's sole recreation, calmed her down somewhat, and Reino kept talking to her.

Meanwhile, Hooker had completed the measurements of the boys and started in with the girls. Alice Maki was the first. Without thinking much about it, he placed the tape measure around her chest.

The room grew quiet as everyone began watching and listening.

"32," Hooker said.

Reino snatched up his pencil and tablet.

"Reino, if you write that down for the yearbook," Alice said, "you'll be eating that pencil."

Hooker suddenly realized that maybe he wasn't the one to be measuring the females and handed the tape to one of the girls.

൵ಌ

Senior Year

I opened our mail box in the post office. There it was, finally, a letter from the University of Michigan. I tore it open and found another form to fill out to declare my major again. Without leaving the post office I filled out the form declaring my new major as architecture, signed it, sealed it in the provided envelope, and took it up to the window.

"Can I buy an airmail stamp for this?"

Arne Millimaki, the Republic postmaster, stared at the address on the envelope. "Ann Arbor? Lemme get this straight. You wanna send this from here to Ann Arbor by *airmail?*"

"Yep. It's gotta get there in a hurry."

"Jeez, lemme think . . . our truck's gotta take it to Marquette for the 9AM flight tomorrow morning. The plane makes two stops before winding up in Lansing late in the afternoon. There ain't, I don't think, any flights from Lansing to Ann Arbor. They gotta put it on another plane to Detroit the next morning and probably truck it over to Ann Arbor. I don't know when it'd get there. Probably faster to send it ground mail. Cheaper, too."

I didn't believe that for a second. "Send it airmail."

༺༻

During the following weeks all of my spare time was taken up getting inside the lead character of J. Oliver Twibbly, the 89-year-old inventor and justice of the peace in the Senior Class Play. I had decided that taking part in the play was wiser than crossing swords with Tank Hankis who still had my final chemistry grade in his clutches.

In Spring the Sap was a study in total wackiness. Mr. Twibbly was working out the kinks in his invention, the Various Machine, designed for various purposes but mainly for the mechanized manufacture of fabricated wallboard out of weeds and garbage. The most fun was building the Various Machine in our manual arts shop. The final product consisted of the chassis of a discarded Maytag washing machine with a stovepipe exhaust protruding from the top. Turning the wringer crank produced a harsh grinding sound like shifting truck gears without engaging the clutch. It was the perfect Various Machine.

In late April, two days before the play date, a dress rehearsal was scheduled in the gym, which doubled as the high-school theater when it wasn't used for basketball.

For me the dress rehearsal involved putting on a stringy white beard such as an old eccentric inventor would sport. Hankis didn't have much patience for details, so several aspects of the play were being handled by Josephine Goodchatter, our high-school language teacher. It was Mrs. Goodchatter who brought the beard to me the afternoon of the rehearsal.

"Gerald, just apply a bit of this glue to the inner side of the beard and press it gently in place. It'll work just fine."

And it did. The rehearsal went off smoothly, and the beard held fast. It was afterward when I tried to remove the beard that there was a problem. It was stuck to my face. Mrs. Goodchatter applied soap and warm water, but that didn't work.

Mr. Hankis came over and looked at the situation. "What kind of glue was it?"

Goodchatter shrugged. "It's just glue. My husband had it in the garage." She produced a half-pint can. "Here it is."

Hankis experimentally tugged on the beard and then checked the label on the can. "Wood glue." He looked hard at Mrs. Goodchatter. "You gave him *WOOD GLUE* to fix a beard on his face?" He shook his head, and Mrs. Goodchatter's lower lip began to quiver.

Hankis looked at the label again. "It's got resins in it. Alcohol might dissolve it, I don't know. May have to go to acetone." He looked at me. "Probably raise hell with your skin. The play is the day after tomorrow. Best thing to do is leave the beard on till after the play, and then we'll work at getting it off." As he thought about getting the beard off he began to chuckle.

My mother stared when I came into the kitchen for supper. "Are you trying to be funny?"

"No."

"Then take that thing off your face."

"I can't"

❧❦

As luck would have it I had a date with Alice Maki that evening for Cokes and cheeseburgers at the Bumblebee Cafe. I knocked on the Maki's back door.

"Are you trying to be funny?" Alice snapped when she opened the door and saw me.

"No."

"Then take that thing off your face."

"I can't"

She turned around and slammed the door shut.

❧❦

The next afternoon Ichabod Schuyler, the school superintendent, was presiding over the 3PM study hall period. He pointed his long bony finger at me in the back row. "Gerald, are you trying to be funny?"

"No, sir."

"Then take that thing off your face."

"I can't, sir."

❧❦

In Spring the Sap proved to be quite a success. The audience–admittedly friends and relatives of the cast–applauded enthusiastically and we gave two curtain calls. Everyone admired my beard including

Ichabod Schuyler, Alice Maki, and my mother.

With the help of a few solvents provided by Mr. Hankis, the beard finally came off along with a generous portion of skin.

Commencement was now less than a month away. My graduation suit arrived from Montgomery Ward, and as I predicted a gorilla could have gotten into it. But my mother, an expert seamstress, pulled it in here, tucked it in there, and the suit fit like a glove just in time for class pictures. Luckily the photographer didn't need a special lens to capture my towering pompadour which could have picked up radio signals on a good day.

Our class rings arrived. Several of the boy's rings quickly disappeared from their fingers to reappear on chains around girls necks. My ring stayed on my finger. I briefly considered offering it to a few girls, but after some thought decided that there wasn't much of a market for my ring.

In the final days I was drafted into the job of Assistant Editor of our yearbook. I checked over our class song–words sung to the tune of April Showers–to make sure that each line had the proper number of syllables. I also made a few witty contributions to the Class Will. Lastly I helped Reino Rovaniemi do the final compilations of the senior class statistics. The girls actually did get on the scale with Bow Wow Bandini naturally topping the chart. However, no bust measurements made it into the yearbook.

◊

In general everything was going well, that is right up to the day I went to the post office, opened our box and found a letter from the University of Michigan.

At last I thought. My acceptance letter from the School of Architecture and Design. I tore it open.

Dear Mr. Harju

Senior Year

It is our pleasure to inform you that you have been accepted as a freshman student at the University of Michigan's College of Engineering . . .

I read that first sentence four times and still couldn't believe it. College of *ENGINEERING? ENGINEERING?* Why wasn't I going to the College of Architecture and Design? What happened to my second application? I crushed the letter in my hand and headed for the door.

Ollie Millimaki leaned out of his little window. "Did'ja ever find out how long it took your airmail letter to get to Ann Arbor?"

Maybe that was it. The plane crashed.

৪০৫৪

I sat in Clarence Hooker's office while he read the letter. Hooker shook his head. "Boy, I dunno. The U. of M. is a big place; I suppose things get misplaced." He scanned the bottom of the letter once more. "They got you all set up, too, which dormitory you'll be living in, where to report for orientation the first week . . . "

"But can I do anything?"

"Well, you could write another letter."

I shook my head. "Letters get lost. This guy in the engineering office, what's his name, Towbridge, who signed the letter, I'm gonna call him up long distance."

Hooker raised his eyebrows. In 1951 when some poor soul reached the end of his rope and really, really had to get something done, then hang the expense, it was time to make a long-distance telephone call.

৪০৫৪

The only place in Republic that had a pay telephone was Hocking's liquor store. Old man Hocking sold liquor but was also a notary public on the side, so long-distance calls were sometimes necessary.

I stood next to the phone with a supply of nickels, dimes and quarters, waiting for the operator to make the connection and tell me how much it would cost.

"Please insert thirty-five cents for three minutes."

I carefully put a quarter and a dime in the slot. The faint ringing sounded like it was coming from Mars. "Mr. Towbridge's office," a tiny, tinny voice said.

"Can I speak to Mr. Towbridge?" I yelled into the phone.

"I'm sorry. He's gone to a meeting."

Nothing was going right. "When will he be back?"

"I really don't know, sir."

"Could he please call me?" I'd just hang around Hocking's store and wait for the call.

"Are you an engineering student with us?"

"Yeah, well, that's the thing. There's been a mistake. I'm supposed to be in architecture, but something got mixed up. I'd like to talk to Mr. Towbridge about it."

"I'm sorry but our office doesn't call students. We only correspond by mail. What's your name?"

I told her and there was a long pause while she looked me up in the file.

"Yes, Gerald, you're all set with us. Did you say there's been a mistake? It would be difficult at this late date to make changes."

"Yes, but listen . . . "

"Your three minutes are up," the operator said. "Please deposit another thirty-five cents to extend the call."

To hell with it. I hung up.

Senior Year

෨෬

As mid-May approached, the days to commencement wound down, igniting a flurry of activity at school. The girl's chorus practiced commencement selections. A speaker was lined up to deliver an address about girding up our loins and looking bravely into the future. A last-minute hang-up with the diplomas resulted in several irate and expensive long-distance calls from Hocking's Liquor to a Grand Rapids printing company. Miss Abigail Wickstock, our high-school music teacher could be found at all hours banging away on the old upright piano in the gym, honing her personal compositions for the processional and recessional. Ichabod Schuyler and Clarence Hooker got into a heated debate on whether the capped-and-gowned seniors should enter the gymnasium according to height, by sex, or alphabetically.

I was also involved. The yearbook still hadn't been put to bed, and I had to chase around town getting more local businesses to pony up for ads so we could meet the printing costs.

All of the seniors were excited, telling one another about post-graduation plans. Some of the girls had lined up stenographer jobs in big cities like Green Bay and Milwaukee. A couple of them realized that they still had a class ring hanging around their neck, and if it was still there after graduation they would be expected to marry the owner of the ring which wasn't in their immediate plans. The ring was covertly returned to its original owner.

I wasn't too enthusiastic about discussing my future which looked somewhat bleak. I had resigned myself to the College of Engineering: four more years of school taking courses I wouldn't get credit for in classrooms with no girls and then trying to find a job that would pay less than a tool and die maker's salary in Milwaukee.

But I had decided to endure it for one semester to satisfy my mother, then drop out of the whole U. of M. thing and head for

Milwaukee to carry out my original plan. The Buick with the exhaust ports in the front fenders and the girls were waiting.

☙❦

Friday, May 25, 1951: Commencement night. I thought I knew how to tie a necktie, but I'd somehow screwed it up. Now I had to stand patiently while my mother performed the operation. How she had mastered the art of tying a man's necktie on someone else's neck was always a mystery.

"You're going to have to learn to do this yourself when you get to Ann Arbor," she muttered, making the final adjustment.

My father, also dressed in his one and only suit, was sitting in his leather easy chair reading the *Mining Journal*.

"Hey, Pop, let's go. It's time." I was driving my parents to commencement in my rattletrap Model A Ford, not a grand way to travel but all we had.

The old man got up with the open newspaper in hand and thrust it at me. "Read this," he said, pointing at an article on an inside page.

"Pop, let's go. We're gonna be late."

"Read it!" he snapped.

I took the paper and looked at the article he was pointing at.

> *Korean Conflict and Soviet Tensions Trigger*
> *High Demand for Engineers*
> *The Korean war and tense relations with Soviet Russia has created an unprecedented demand for engineers. Recruiters for companies such as North American Aviation, Boeing, Lockheed, and General Electric are now posted in the halls of colleges and universities around the country, enticing graduating engineers with sky-high*

starting salaries. The need for engineers is so great that incoming female freshmen are now considering a career in engineering.

I handed the newspaper back to my father. "Don't throw the paper away. I want to save that."

Driving to the high-school gym I was thinking: yeah, okay, I can get in on the ground floor. First thing Monday morning I need to go over to Hocking's and call Towbridge's office at the U. of M., just talk to his secretary and tell her everything is just fine now the way it is.

❦

The seniors assembled in the small hallway leading into the gym. It had been decided that when the processional music began that we were entering by pairs matched up by height. Bow Bow Bandini was at my side, scowling as she tried to remember what side the cap tassel was supposed to be on before she received her diploma.

"Hi, Barbara," I said warmly, clasping her hand in a gesture of friendship.

Bow Wow jerked her hand away. "Whaddaya think yer doin'?"

The old piano that Miss Wickstock was going to use for the processional and recessional had suddenly given up the ghost, and someone had to bring in a portable phonograph. A scratchy 78 rpm record of "Pomp and Circumstance" began playing, and we started to march in.

The record began skipping, playing the same two bars over and over. The marching seniors fell out of step, and some of them began cursing under their breath.

It sounded okay to me I thought. In fact, it sounded just fine.

❦

COLLEGE GIRLS 101

September, 1951. My mother snuffled back a tear sitting on the edge of my bed as I packed for Ann Arbor. I was about to start my freshman year at the University of Michigan.

"I'll miss you, but I'm so glad you're going," she said. "College will teach you to become a gentleman, and how to dress nicely, and I know you'll meet some refined women." She blew her nose, then added, "And maybe you'll finally learn to chew with your mouth closed."

I soon discovered that student priorities in Michigan's engineering college didn't include being a gentleman nor dressing nicely. In the places where I ate my meals chewing with your mouth closed was optional. Mom was right about one thing, though. I did manage to meet some refined women. Well, I guess a few of them were refined.

ℰ)(ℛ

I arrived in Ann Arbor by train, dressed in my high-school graduation suit, carrying one suitcase filled with four shirts, three pairs of pants, assorted socks, and six pairs of underwear, all with my name printed in indelible ink.

The university dictated that all freshmen were to live in a

dormitory, so I became a resident of the Allen Rumsey House in the West Quadrangle. The lounge at Allen Rumsey boasted a large 12-inch television set, if you can imagine.

The first Monday was the beginning of freshmen orientation week, a time to get acquainted with the campus, take physical exams, and register for classes. I had explicit, written instructions guiding me through every minute for five straight days. At 8AM sharp I was scheduled to report to a room on the second floor of the Michigan Union building.

The Union had the atmosphere of a gentlemen's private club, with dark wood paneling and large crystal chandeliers, a proper setting for old fogies to sit around in the heavy, leather-upholstered chairs and read the financial news. But this morning the Union was teeming with freshmen scurrying in all directions. The second-floor room was already crowded with young men.

My graduation suit was considerably more formal than the prevailing dress code. Many of the guys were wearing curious-looking white-suede shoes. These white-shoe people tended to talk only to one another–some sort of club, I figured. I later found out that the shoes were called white bucks–very much in style and very expensive.

A handsome, deeply tanned person dressed in a crisply starched white shirt, gray flannel slacks with razor-sharp creases, and, of course, white bucks marched up to the podium at the front of the room. He held up his hand for silence.

"Good morning. I'm Jack Radcliff–Engineering '53. I'll be your orientation leader throughout the week." As he grinned, the light from an ornate chandelier glistened off of his toothpaste-ad, perfect teeth.

"All of you are Engineering '55. This week is designed to acquaint you with the areas of the campus where you'll be spending most of your time. You'll notice that there are no women in the group . . . we are, after all, engineers." Then he added with a confidential half-smile, half-leer, "But that doesn't mean your social life will

College Girls 101

wither. Twice a day we'll be taking *mixer breaks*, so you'll have plenty of opportunity to meet women."

Radcliff let that revelation sink in as he fished out a knobby briarwood pipe, filled it with tobacco from a soft leather pouch, and expertly lit it with a gold lighter. Some of the other white-buck guys immediately brought out pipes and began to stoke them up.

"Before we get started this morning," Radcliff continued, "do you know what you *are*, as of this moment? Anybody?"

No one spoke up.

"You're *Michigan Wolverines*!" Radcliff cried. "And when we walk around the campus this week I want you all to throw your shoulders back and show some Wolverine pride! Let's go!" He quickly headed for the door.

A Michigan Wolverine. I savored the thought as we followed Radcliff out of the room. I had never seen a wolverine, but I'd heard they were bad news, able to beat the crap out of everything else in the woods. I threw my shoulders back.

Radcliff gave us a quick tour of the Union, the billiard room on the second floor and the barber shop, swimming pool, and four-lane bowling alley in the basement.

Outside, Radcliff brought the group to a halt at the Michigan Union front entrance on State Street. "I'm going to start your education right now." He pointed up the steps at the Union. "The Union is an exclusive club for Michigan *men*. It's *your* club. When you bring a woman into the Union you *must* use the side door over to the right. *Women are not allowed to use the main entrance of the Union.* Understood?"

It made perfect sense and we nodded wisely. After all, we couldn't let just *anyone* walk into our club–especially through the front door. In two columns, we stepped out smartly down South University Avenue, trailing great plumes of pipe-tobacco smoke in our wake.

Northern Tales No. 5

Over on East University Avenue we toured the engineering buildings. Deep in the bowels of the West Engineering building we were shown huge machines that engineers used to break things that other engineers had designed. We viewed the large water tank that naval-architecture engineering students used for sailing and testing boat models.

After visiting the physics buildings we proceeded over to the Michigan League, the women's equivalent of the Union. Radcliff ushered us into a large cafeteria whereupon he immediately struck up a conversation with a good-looking blonde. After a few words he came back over and gathered us into a huddle.

"Okay men, this is our first mixer break," he said quietly. He pointed to a large group of girls sitting at tables near the far wall. "See those women? Go over there, pick one out, find out what she wants to drink, and get her name and telephone number. We've only got thirty minutes, so get to it." Having issued orders to his troops, Radcliff returned to the blonde–the female orientation group leader–and led her to an empty table.

The operation was clear. We had established a beachhead and our mission was to storm out and engage the enemy.

The white-bucks clearly had more stomach for this, whipping out address books as they quickly approached the girls. By and by, the rest of us tentatively followed.

I was paralyzed with fear. The few girls I had dated in the Upper Peninsula, I'd known for years. On occasion, a few of us studs would drive to neighboring towns to cruise around on the pretext that we were bored with the Republic girls. It amounted to nothing more than slowing down and making suggestive comments to the girls on the sidewalk as we drove by. None of us had ever mustered up the nerve to actually make a date with a strange girl.

By the time I edged over to the freshmen girls, all the good-looking ones had been taken. The ones left were in a peevish mood

College Girls 101

because they hadn't been selected. I gingerly approached a sour-looking, round-faced girl sitting by herself.

"Uh . . . hi," I said glibly.

"Don't feel obligated," she snapped.

"Whut?"

"Don't feel obligated to pick me up."

"Oh . . . no . . . no . . . it's fine with me. I'm happy t'pick you up." *That didn't come out right.*

"This whole mixer thing stinks," she said waspishly. "Why don't they quit wasting our time and just get this orientation business over with? I've got more important things to do . . . like getting over to Slater's Bookstore." She drummed her fingers impatiently on the empty table.

I remembered that I was supposed to ask her what she wanted to drink. " Can I buy you a cuppa coffee . . . a Coke . . . anything'?"

"Well . . . as long as I'm stuck here for awhile . . . I'll take a strawberry sundae."

Strawberry sundae?–damn, one with expensive taste. I went up to the counter and got the sundae, plus a cup of coffee for myself. The coffee was steaming hot, and I almost poured some into the saucer to cool it off–U. P. style–but caught myself. With a sour look, the girl ate the sundae in silence.

Radcliff came over and snapped his fingers, indicating the mixer was over. The men got up and followed him out. Neither the sundae-eater nor I had a burning desire to exchange names and telephone numbers.

"I got *two* names and phone numbers," said one of the white-bucks.

"I got *three,*" cried another.

"Excellent!" Radcliff exclaimed, closely inspecting the two with an appraising eye, no doubt considering them as potential candidates for his Sigma Nu fraternity. He'd let it slip during the morning tour that hard-hitting ladies men were in strong demand at Sigma Nu.

We toured the chemistry building, then broke for lunch. I trudged back to the dormitory dining hall where I was introduced to the infamous West-Quad lunchtime fare of grilled-cheese sandwiches and tomato soup.

The sandwiches had the texture of old sweat socks. What I didn't realize was–this being Monday–they were relatively fresh and tender. The survivors would congeal into a truly impenetrable mass before being served again on Friday.

At two in the afternoon the Radcliff team once again intercepted a female orientation group in the Michigan League cafeteria. This time I screwed up my courage and moved in faster, snaring a busty brunette with pouty lips.

"Hi . . . can I get you a cup of coffee or a Coke?" I rattled off nervously.

She bathed me with a fetching smile. "Why, yes," she said in a syrupy Southern drawl. "A cup of coffee would be nice."

This was more like it. I briskly brought two coffees over and sat down. The muscles in my jaw ached from the grin frozen on my face, advertising that I was a very congenial fellow who she should get to know better.

She took a delicate sip of coffee. "Your orientation group is pre-law, is that right?"

"What's that?"

"Ya'll are going to be lawyers, aren't you?"

"Oh, no. We're gonna be engineers."

Her smile evaporated. "Oh . . . dear . . . ah'm sorry. No . . . no . . . ah mean ah would have sworn that Gloria–she's our group leader–said that ya'll were going to be lawyers." She lowered her eyes, gazing into her coffee mug as she attempted to mask her disappointment.

My mind frantically rummaged around for something brilliant to say to salvage the conversation. Finally, in desperation I blurted

College Girls 101

out, "So, what are *you* gonna major in? Heh, heh." *Brilliant.*

"Oh . . . ah haven't rightly decided. Ah expect to be spending most of my time entertaining my future husband's clients. Ah haven't seen anything like that in the course catalogs, though."

She stared intently at each of the boys in Radcliff's orientation group, trying to determine if there were any budding Einsteins among us. "Ah'll give it more thought later in the week when ah register for classes. Right now ah've got to think about which sororities ah want to rush."

My mind went totally blank. How do you respond to career goals like that? I parboiled my upper lip taking a huge gulp of hot coffee in the hope that a jolt of caffeine would inspire me. Nothing. For several minutes we just sat there like two lumps.

Finally, she stood up. "It's been real nice talkin' to ya'll, but ah think ah'll wait for the group outside." She hurried out the door.

಄ಐ

Before dinner that night, I told my troubles to my roommate.

"What am I gonna do?" I moaned. "I can't think of anything to say to these girls at the mixer breaks and this's gonna go on all week!"

Dick Buttram was in the middle of our room, pounding the floor with his feet, practicing his rapid-fire, high-stepping marching exercises–knees thrashing upward toward his chin, like pistons. He was a tuba player in the University of Michigan Marching Band and had to get his legs in shape for the band's trademark 180-steps-per-minute march used when entering the football stadium.

He stopped and mopped his face with a towel. "Had the same problem myself during Orientation Week last year. "You need a script."

"A script?"

"Yeah. You'll never see the same girl twice, unless you wanna make a date, right?"

"I guess so."

"So you write a script of what you're gonna say to a girl, memorize it, and tell them all the same thing. Sprinkle in a few questions to show you're interested in them. Once you get the hang of it, it's easy–you don't even have to think. Don't make it too long, though. Keep it short enough so you can talk to two or three women in a half-hour."

Pure genius. That night I stayed up into the wee hours composing my dialogue.

ଛଔ

On Tuesday after enduring an all-morning physical exam, I rushed over to the West-Quad dining room for lunch. Creamed chipped beef on toast was featured–commonly referred to by veteran West Quadders as SOS. To me, it tasted no worse than deer-camp food. I enthusiastically wolfed it down and went up to my room to pour over my girl-script before the afternoon orientation.

At the two o'clock mixer the freshmen males frantically bolted over to the group of waiting girls. Even the most mild-mannered now realized there was only a split-second's difference between talking to a beauty queen and some plain-Jane also-ran.

By the time I got to the girls' table I found the pickings pretty lean, but no matter. I needed the opportunity to work the kinks out of my script, and it would be easier with a less-demanding subject.

I moved in on a skinny girl with heavy, horn-rimmed glasses.

"I've seen you before," I stated flatly. "You were one of the finalists in the Marquette County Fair Beauty Contest last fall."

She quickly took off her glasses and began massaging the imprints from the bridge of her nose. Buttram was right; you could dish out any amount of outrageous flattery to a plain-looking girl and she'd swallow it hook, line, and sinker.

"Aha! It *was* you," I cried, adlibbing masterfully. "I was right, now that I see you without your glasses."

She shook her head reluctantly and gave me a timid smile, while furiously finger-combing her hair. "No . . . it wasn't me. I'm from Grand Rapids. I don't even know where Marquette County is."

"It's in Upper Michigan . . . that's where I'm from." I introduced myself. "You must have a long-lost twin sister up there, heh, heh, heh."

It was an excellent start, but I had to move along since I had a lengthy agenda. "Would you like something? The coffee here is pretty good." I had learned not to suggest refreshment choices–too expensive and time-consuming.

I brought the coffee over and buzzed through my list of bright quips and probing questions that I'd organized the night before. Just before the half-hour was up I whipped out a slip of paper and a fountain pen and slid them in front of her. "If you don't mind putting down your name and telephone number, I thought we could get together some night and I could tell you more about Upper Michigan."

She smiled again, nodded her head, and wrote down her name and number. I said goodbye and strode confidently over to the door, just in time to join Radcliff and the rest of the group.

෩෨

On Wednesday morning we registered for classes. I found myself stuck with five eight-o'clocks, not exactly an auspicious beginning. But my spirits lifted at the mid-morning mixer break. While I had successfully tested the validity of Buttram's scripted approach yesterday, today I had to work on timing.

Covertly maneuvering to the front of our group as we went through the League-cafeteria door, I quickly snagged a good-looking blonde. Cutting out some of the more mundane dialogue, as well as questions that might require long, complicated answers, I had her name and phone number in less than fifteen minutes. Spotting a lone brunette who had already bought her own coffee–a lucky break–I bid the blonde an abrupt goodbye and moved over to the brunette's table. By the time the half-hour was up I also had her name and number. *Two girls in thirty minutes.* At this rate, I might easily corner the market on freshmen women.

❧

On Thursday, following an early-morning tour of the Intramural Sports Building and the football stadium, our orientation group hiked back to the League for the ten-o'clock mixer break, arriving a few minutes early. I had already snagged a table when I saw *her* at the door.

She was wearing a baby blue cashmere sweater that radiated its own light, bathing her in a soft glow. Shoulder-length, Rita Hayworth-like red hair and large, hazel eyes fringed with thick, dark lashes.

The more-experienced white-bucks in our group also spotted her, and sucked in a collective hot breath as they made a beeline for her.

A few short days ago I wouldn't, in my wildest dreams, have approached such a woman, but competition breeds guts. Struggling for traction on the tile floor, I outlegged the other pursuers and motioned her to my table.

"I've seen you before," I purred, launching into my now-well-polished opening salvo as I held her chair. "You were one of the finalists in the Marquette County Fair Beauty Contest last fall, weren't you?"

Obviously accustomed to such wanton flattery, she simply smiled and shook her head, waiting for me to continue. I silently congratulated myself for having the foresight to write the script. Now

College Girls 101

it was paying off big. The names and numbers of the other girls could be discarded–mere pawns in rehearsal for the real thing–*the girl of my dreams*.

I quickly produced two cups of coffee and loosened her up with brave tales of my early years in the Upper Peninsula–hunting the mighty deer, trapping ferocious muskrat, and catching elusive brook trout.

I spent the entire half-hour with her, no need to talk to others. At a quarter past the hour it was time to switch the discussion to my career plans. I explained that I was going to become an aerodynamicist (I'd looked the word up the night before) and specialize in the design of supersonic (I'd also looked *that* up) aircraft. I offered to explain the theory of supersonic flight to her. My bluff paid off–she declined, laughingly claiming that she wouldn't understand a word of it. I carefully inserted questions here and there as Buttram had instructed and paid rapt attention to her answers.

Her name was Bernice. She was from Flint and intended to major in literature. She had never been to the Upper Peninsula and thought that my stories were fascinating–especially told with my "cute" accent. Would I tell her more about the place?

"We're almost out of time," I explained, whipping out my brand-new pocket address book with one hand and producing a fountain pen with the other, "but why don't we get together this weekend?"

Then, I had an even better idea. "Tomorrow, the freshmen have to pick up their season football tickets at Waterman. Why don't we go together and get seats next to each other?"

Her eyes sparkled, and she clapped her hands in delight. "Oooh, that would be wonderful." She lightly touched my hand, sending shivers of through my body.

This one definitely had possibilities.

෴

November, 1951. Seven weeks later my life had become total misery. I endured classes run by ruthless professors, wolfed down unidentifiable substances in the West Quad dining room, groped with riddling mathematical equations into the wee hours, and passed out on a thin, lumpy mattress every night.

One evening at 9PM I closed my solid geometry text, put away my slide rule, stood up from my desk, and stretched the kinks out of my back. *The FBI in Peace and War* was ready to start on TV, so I headed for the first-floor lounge.

I passed Nathan McCool, resident of room 304, standing in his doorway. McCool was a senior in business administration and was known in the Allen Rumsey dorm as "the fixer." He had contacts in every women's dormitory on campus and at a moments notice could fix you up with a date. No one knew exactly why he did it. One opinion was that he was serving a self-apprenticeship and planned to start a high-priced escort service following graduation. McCool had already contacted all of the freshmen at Allen Rumsey about getting them dates. Up to my ears in homework and still smarting from the disaster with Bernice, I'd turned him down.

"When's the last time you had a date with a girl?" McCool asked.

"It's been awhile," I admitted morosely.

The romance with Bernice from Flint had died a slow, agonizing death weeks ago. Our first encounter during Orientation Week had set the pace. From then on, every time I opened my mouth she expected me to whip off scintillating witticisms. Swamped with homework with no time to prepare fresh dialog, I soon ran out of clever material and clammed up. With her looks, Bernice never needed a reason to develop conversational skills. We had gotten adjoining seats in the football stadium, but at the first home game we spent three excruciatingly silent hours together. After that she kept inventing excuses for not going to the rest of the games. I never saw her again.

McCool gave me a slow, easy smile. "Want to take out a nice

girl this Saturday?"

"Ahhh . . . I don't think so," I replied timidly. "I gotta big English theme to turn in on Monday morning . . . a chemistry blue book on Tuesday ..."

McCool's eyes darted up and down the hallway, then leaned closer, indicating that what he was about to say was in strictest confidence. "I can fix you up with a *sorority* girl," he whispered.

My pulse blipped. How could that be? Only fraternity men took out sorority women. Dormitory men took out dormitory women. It was a well-understood caste system that was rarely violated. On the other hand it would be a tremendous boost to my image–to say nothing of my ego–if word got around Allen Rumsey that I had dated a sorority woman.

McCool caught the spark of interest and pressed on. "You're a shy guy around women, am I right? Well, the girl I have in mind is a good match for you–an excellent conversationalist and doesn't mind the strong silent type. All you have to do is nod your head and smile."

☙❧

At six-thirty p.m. on Saturday night I stood in front of the wall mirror in my room nervously preparing for the blind date that McCool had arranged.

Dick Beaudry, my next door neighbor in room 311, looked at me incredulously from the doorway. "A necktie with airplanes flying across it?"

I finished putting the knot in my prized a necktie, a fine piece of six-inch-wide rayon material with a formation of B-17 Flying Fortresses in flight across the blue sky.

"Is that the only tie you have?"

"No, but it's the best one."

"At least put a Windsor knot in it," Beaudry advised. Beaudry came from Grosse Pointe, a posh Detroit suburb, and had become the third-floor de facto advisor on wardrobe and cultural matters.

"What's a Winser knot?"

"Ah . . . never mind. Actually, that knot you made goes rather well with the tie. So, where are you taking this sorority girl?"

"There's a brand-new Gary Cooper movie at the State Theater . . . *Distant Drums*."

Beaudry's jaw dropped. "You're taking a sorority girl to a *cowboys and Indians* movie?"

"No good, huh? What else is there?" I asked.

"For one thing, *The Seagull* is playing at the Lydia Mendelssohn Theater in the League building."

"*The Seagull*?"

"Yes. The comedy by Anton Chekhov."

"A comedy?" I exclaimed, putting on my suit coat. "I like comedies. I haven't seen a good funny movie since I left home."

"This isn't a movie," Beaudry explained. "It's a four-act play."

"Oh, yeah? The only play I've ever seen was one I had a part in. Our senior class at Republic High School put it on, and I played the lead character."

"Yes . . . well . . . a word of caution." Beaudry said, eyeing me carefully and speaking slowly. "If you go to *The Seagull*, don't laugh unless you hear the rest of the audience laughing."

ೞ಄

A chill wind whipped through the large trees overhanging Washtenaw Avenue as I hurried over to the Delta Tau sorority house.

At the last minute, I'd pulled out my girl-script used so successfully during Orientation Week and refreshed my memory on the clever dialog. If she was as good a talker as McCool claimed, there was easily enough conversational material to get me through

College Girls 101

the evening–especially if we were watching a play.

Three-story white columns guarded the tall oak front door of the Delta Tau sorority house. It was a huge, brick colonial-style mansion set well back from the street. I knocked on the door, bruising my knuckles on the solid wood, then noticed the doorbell and rang it. A muted chime ding-donged off in the distance.

The door sighed reluctantly as it opened. A pretty girl smiled politely at me. "Who is it you wish to see?"

My mind went blank. I hastily dug the piece of paper out of my pocket. "Eleanor Ridgerock," I said.

She opened the door wider, momentarily glancing at my necktie. "Come in, please."

The foyer was larger than the whole first floor of our house in Republic. A wide, richly stained wooden staircase curved gracefully up to a spacious second-floor landing. A magnificent crystal chandelier, the size of a Chevrolet, reached down from the soaring ceiling, casting soft light on oriental rugs artfully positioned on the hardwood floor. Imperious-looking middle-aged women–influential alumnae of Delta Tau, no doubt–stared disapprovingly at me from dark oil paintings on the walls.

The girl who let me in pressed one of several buttons on a wall-mounted panel. "Won't you take a seat?" she said. "Eleanor will be down shortly." I sat down gingerly on an antique chair upholstered in a heavy brocade.

Two fraternity-type fellows entered without ringing the doorbell. They punched buttons on the panel with practiced familiarity and sat down next to me. Each wore a navy blue sports coat, gray flannel slacks, and white-buck shoes. They stared at my tie.

Several girls passed through the foyer–all beautiful and exquisitely dressed. My blind date was certain to be a doll. *This one would definitely have possibilities.*

But would my mind freeze up like it did on the last date with

Bernice? With effort, I got a grip on myself, reasoning that after all, with the girl-script fresh in my mind, I should handle the situation easily.

Footsteps on the staircase echoed in the foyer. I looked up, froze, and blinked my eyes several times. A bear was coming down the stairs–in high heels. The bear came up to me, stopped, and looked me up and down, eyes pausing briefly on my necktie.

"Hi, I'm Eleanor."

She was a very large girl wearing a full-length, dark brown mink coat. She towered over me by several inches, and judging from the width of her shoulders, she probably outweighed me by at least thirty pounds–maybe more, it was hard to tell with the fur coat. I scrambled out of the chair and stood up.

Looking down critically at the top of my head, she said, "Just a minute. I'll be right back." She clacked back up the stairs in her heels and moments later padded down, somewhat shorter now in dark blue tennis shoes. She was still about six-one.

Eleanor had nice, even features–lean, square jaw, long straight nose, and piercing blue eyes–fairly attractive if she had been a man. She could easily have passed for John Wayne's twin sister.

I squeaked out my name as she grabbed my hand with a bone-crushing shake. The girl-script was useless. There was no way I could look her in the eye with a straight face and say that I thought she was one of the finalists in the Marquette County Fair Beauty Contest. The log-splitting contest, maybe.

"Excuse the shoes," she said. "Our sorority date coordinator always tries to line me up with guys who are at least six-four. I guess your dorm contact didn't get the word."

I shook my head, making a mental note to set Nathan McCool's hair on fire.

"So where're we headed?" Eleanor asked as we walked down the sidewalk.

College Girls 101

"There's a play at the Lydia Mendelssohn," I replied. *"The Seagull."*

"Oh, yes . . . by Chekhov," she replied enthusiastically. "I'm a contemporary-literature major. I'm glad you picked *The Seagull*. It's a favorite of mine. I hope they have a believable cast tonight. I saw an off-Broadway version of it last year, and would you believe that the fellow who played Constantine Gavrilovich Treplev had a *New York accent*? He sounded like a cab driver." She chuckled at the absurdity of it all.

McCool had been right about one thing. She was a strong conversationalist. The only trouble was I didn't know what the hell she was conversing about. Should I try to fake it? No–I was too ignorant to try anything devious.

I said, "This . . . Constantine Gavri . . . Gavri . . . whatever his name is. He almost sounds like a Russian or something."

There was a short silence. "Yes . . . Russian. The whole play takes place in Russia," she replied in measured tones. "In fact, *all* of Chekhov's plays take place in Russia."

"Oh, I see . . . that's great. Are there spies in it?"

Eleanor half-snorted as she tried to suppress a laugh. "Spies, that's good. There aren't any spies in Chekhov's plays. You see, they all take place around the turn of the century . . . before the Russian revolution." She paused. "You're not familiar with Chekhov's plays at all, are you?"

"I've never been to a play in my life, except one we put on in high school," I said truthfully.

She was astonished. "You've *never* seen a play?"

I shook my head.

She stared at the sidewalk intently. "Oh . . . well . . . I suppose you read novels though, right?"

I smiled and nodded enthusiastically. A copy of Mickey Spillane's *I, The Jury* had just completed the rounds on the third floor of Allen

Rumsey, each guy getting one hour to read the marked-up, steamy sections. "Yeah. I love novels."

She brightened up. "Have you read Tolstoy's works?"

"'Tolstoy's Works,' . . . I guess I missed that one."

"No . . . no . . . I meant novels written by Leo Tolstoy."

I shook my head again.

"How about Sinclair Lewis?" she asked.

"Ahhh . . . nope."

"Aldous Huxley . . . *Brave New World*?" she said hopefully.

"No."

Her face hardened with defeat. "You're an *engineer*, aren't you?"

"Yeah, that's right. How'd you know?"

ಸಂಒ

The Seagull was *not* a comedy. In fact, it was a tragedy since I missed a brand-new Gary Cooper western because of it. For three hours, people with jaw-breaking names stood around onstage making stupid conversation. A couple of them were writers, serving to remind me that I still had my English 11 theme due on Monday morning. The fourth act mercifully ground to a halt when the main character committed suicide. The only seagull in the play was dead, most likely dying from boredom.

But Eleanor enjoyed the play, and on the walk back to the sorority house, she carried on at some length about the unfulfilled love between Constantine Gavrilovich and Nina Mikhailovna and the symbolism of the seagull. I tagged along with a tight grin on my face, nodding from time to time. I didn't ask her what symbolism was; the seagull looked just plain dead to me.

At the Delta Tau doorway she smiled and I got another firm handshake. "I had a nice time tonight and really enjoyed the play. Thank you very much."

She looked at me appraisingly. "Can I give you some advice? Don't wind up like the rest of the engineers I've seen around campus who graduate after four years only knowing gear ratios and tensile strengths. Pick up some good literature and read. You might really like it." She turned and went inside.

I strode down Washtenaw Avenue deep in thought. Eleanor Ridgerock was right. As long as I was in college I ought to broaden myself. First thing Monday morning I'd pop down to Slater's Bookstore and pick out something from the literature section to expand my mind.

It was getting late and I picked up the pace. The State Theater was having a midnight showing of *Distant Drums*.

ಸಿ)ಲ

August, 1953. I sat up in bed with a start. Someone was calling my name. The clock on the dresser said 9:30. I never slept that late, but I'd completed my two final exams the day before. My sophomore year was officially over, but I'd had to attend summer session in order to make up math deficiencies. During the summer I'd rented a room on Jefferson Street.

The landlady was calling from the stairwell. "You have a telephone call."

I stumbled down the stairs, trying to shake the cobwebs out of my head as I picked up the receiver. "Hello."

"Jer . . . this is Sternitzky." Letch Sternitzky, a friend from the spring semester drafting class had also attended summer session. "How'd you do on your finals?"

"Okay on the engineering statics, but only so-so on calculus."

"Well, that's water under the bridge. Tonight's your last night in town, isn't it?"

"Yeah. I'm leaving in the morning."

"You taking your girl out tonight?"

"Yeah. Ruth and I are probably just gonna get a bite to eat and take in a movie–maybe *Stalag 17* at the Michigan Theater." That summer I'd been dating Ruth Grimbsy, a 21-year-old education senior. Ruth was a bit on the reserved side and a year older than me, but she was good looking and I was developing a taste for older women. *This one definitely had possibilities* .

"*Stalag 17*?" Letch exclaimed incredulously. "The last night with your girl and you're taking her to a *war* movie? Not too classy. Wanna hear a better idea?"

"What's that?"

"I been taking care of somebody's house while they're on summer vacation. An engineering prof and his family who live out on Huron River Drive. Pretty fancy place. I figure we could double date, bring the girls out here to the house, and listen to some music."

"The owner lets you bring people over?"

"They're outta town till next week. Who's to know?"

ಸಿಂಡ

"Is that really a TV set?" I asked. I had no idea TV screens were made that big.

"Yep, a twenty-one-incher," Letch declared proudly. "But it's more than that. It's a Sylvania Monticello console combo. TV . . . AM-FM radio . . . 3-speed phono . . . the works."

"Look at this rug," Ruth exclaimed. "It goes all the way to the walls."

Ruth and I and Letch and his girl, Gail, had just entered the quietly elegant living room of the home where Letch was house-sitting for the summer. Letch went to the console and turned on the TV. Half a minute later, the twenty-one-inch screen blazed to life. A gigantic Ed Sullivan had just introduced a team of seals decked out in New

College Girls 101

York Knicks uniforms. We all watched intently as the seals cleverly passed a basketball from nose to nose.

A commercial came on, and Letch turned the TV off and flipped on the phonograph. "Why don't we put on some music instead?" He stacked several long-playing records onto the automatic turntable. "Ebb Tide" drifted across the room.

"Anybody care for a little drink?" Letch asked from a small bar against the wall. He had produced a tall frosty glass filled with ice cubes clinking together invitingly.

"Whatever you're having," Gail said provocatively. Letch grinned and brought up a large bottle of rum from below the bar.

"Do you have any Coca-Cola?" Ruth asked.

"Sure, but why don't you let me put a touch of rum in it. Makes a great drink . . . can't even taste the rum. After all, we gotta celebrate getting through summer session, don't we?"

"Just a tiny bit then," Ruth said tentatively.

"I'll take the same," I said.

Letch poured a large shot of rum and some Coke into each of the four glasses and passed the drinks around. He motioned to the Sylvania. "If you really wanna appreciate the fidelity of this sound system, you gotta get down next to the speakers . . . right here on the floor."

We all sat down on the carpet in front of the huge console and sipped our drinks. "Getting to Know You" drifted softly out of the speakers. I put my arm around Ruth, and she leaned her head back onto my shoulder. The memory of the Calculus II final began to fade.

Another record slid down the automatic spindle onto the turntable, but for awhile no sound came from the speakers. Then, a soft syncopated beat emerged, followed by a haunting melody played by a single oboe. It was Ravel's "Bolero." Never having heard it before, I had no idea that it was one of the most seductive pieces of music ever written.

Other instruments joined in, supporting the oboe in repeating the melody. The volume grew and the beat became more restless. By now we had finished our drinks and all four of us were lying on the carpet, absorbed with the hypnotic melody. I leaned over Ruth. We looked into each other's eyes and kissed. Not an ordinary kiss but soft and lingering. It had the faintly exotic essence of rum and Dentyne chewing gum.

I didn't have to look up to know what was going on with Letch and Gail. I could hear the heavy breathing.

The melody, now led by violins, kept repeating, not monotonously, but continually inching upward in volume and tempo, promising the listener future exotic pleasures.

Ruth, eyes closed, was lying on her back on the carpet. We kissed again, longer, harder, with more urgency. I came up for air, but she put her arms around my neck and pulled me back down again. As we kissed, I opened my eyes, briefly glancing at the beige carpet. It had become sand on an Oahu beach, and the music was warm seawater washing over our bodies. I was Burt Lancaster, and Ruth was Deborah Kerr.

Led by throbbing trumpets, "Bolero" engulfed the room, converging on some unknown but inevitable destination. I placed my hand on Ruth's breast.

She sat bolt upright on the carpet.

"*WHAT* DO YOU THINK YOU'RE DOING?"

Ruth scrambled to her feet. "I see . . . you thought you could pour a little rum in me, take advantage–here on the rug of all places–and then leave town. Well, you got another think coming, buster. C'mon, Gail. Let's go."

Letch and Gail, in the midst of an advanced stage of unbuttoning, sat up. Feeling obligated to side with Ruth, Gail buttoned up and got to her feet. The front door slammed shut just as "Bolero" reached its climactic ending.

College Girls 101

※

There once was a Union maid,
Who never was afraid,
Of goons and ginks and company finks
And deputy sheriffs who made the raids;

Led by two acoustic guitars, the crowd in the living room of Lester House–a women's co-op–were singing old union songs and various other protest dittys. These songs were not on your Lucky Strike Hit Parade.

In my junior year I'd elected to stretch my dollars by moving into a co-op house. Owen House–a once-stately mansion on Oakland–now looked like a Nevada bordello. The resident multinational students were responsible for maintaining the house, and last summer a select group of liberal free thinkers, no doubt primed by large quantities of beer, painted the outside with colors of their choice.

My job at Owen House was furnace tender, responsible for keeping the ancient furnace going by shoveling coal into an equally ancient stoker. During January and February the stoker had to be filled four times a day, and during those months there was little hope that the furnace tender could ever scrub the coal dust out of his pores.

"Union Maid" was the final song in a medley urging the downtrodden workers to rise up against the cruelty and indifference of greedy capitalist bosses. If Joe McCarthy had been at Lester House that night, he would have run out of paper taking names. But I wasn't concerned about McCarthy blacklists. I was looking for women.

It was long over between Ruth and me. I had called her several times after the breast-touching incident but couldn't even get a coffee date.

So after weeks of dealing with differential equations, thermodynamic heat engines, and a hungry coal stoker I was on the prowl for female companionship. She could even be a communist for all I cared.

There was a break in the singing as refreshments were served–canned sardines on toothpicks, peanut butter and Ritz cracker sandwiches, and some kind of cheap wine that came in gallon jugs.

I surveyed the women, knowing that the ten dollars in my pocket would enable me to treat any one of them to a far more lavish experience than a co-op hootenany.

I bent over a woman sitting cross-legged on the carpet. "Hi, my name is Jerry . . . "

She produced an unlit cigarette out of nowhere and held it in her fingers. "Got a light?"

I dug out a wooden kitchen match, the accepted co-op cigarette lighter. I looked around for someplace to strike it. Nothing.

She snatched the match from my hand and scratched the match head with her thumbnail, setting it ablaze. "Thanks," she said dryly, turning away to resume her conversation with one of the guitar players.

That's okay, I thought–plenty of other fish in the sea. In fact, two fairly attractive fish were talking near the refreshment table, which now held a large, metal mixing bowl filled with punch.

Employing my most engaging smile I said, "Hi, can I get you two a cup of punch?" The two women looked at me for a moment, then nodded.

I quickly filled three paper cups with the yellowish punch and handed them each one. I took a gulp of mine.

My throat was immediately paralyzed. "What *is* this?" I wheezed. My eyes began to water.

One of the woman took a sip. "Oh, it's that stuff the guys over in Nakamura House mix up," she remarked offhandedly. "Grapefruit juice and grain alcohol. Somebody should get after them. It's a bit strong."

The other one tossed her punch off with one gulp, turned to me, and said, "Maybe you can settle the argument we're having. Where was Joe Hill executed: Utah or Colorado?"

"Joe Hill?" I croaked.

"You know . . . the famous Wobbly organizer."

"Wobbly?" *I* was feeling a little wobbly.

"Wobbly–the IWW–the Industrial Workers of the World. You're new to co-ops, aren't you?" she stated. The guitars started up again and the two left me to join the singers.

It was clear that I hadn't absorbed enough co-op culture to socialize effectively, so I decided to leave and drown my sorrows with skim milk and a peanut butter sandwich at Owen House.

As I proceeded to the front door, head down, I ran smack into a woman–a full-body collision with all four of our arms locking up.

At first glance she appeared to be older than the rest–perhaps the Lester housemother–but looking more closely as we disengaged, I realized it wasn't age wrinkles on her forehead. *It was coal dust!*

She also looked at *my* face with interest. "You're a furnace tender," she said softly.

"Over at Owen House. You are too, aren't you?"

"Right here at Lester."

"The weather's finally warming up." I knew that she would fully appreciate the significance of that remark.

She smiled, the spider webs of coal dust cracking around her mouth. "Isn't it wonderful? I only have to fill the stoker three times a day now."

"Been having much trouble with rocks in the coal?" My dialogue now flowed effortlessly.

"Oh, yes." Her laughter tinkled like a fairy's bell. "But I'm almost out of shear pins." The coal was liberally laced with rocks, frequently snapping the shear pin on the stoker worm gear. It was the job of the furnace tender to replace the pin.

"Almost out? I make my own."

Her breathing became rapid. She looked into my eyes and licked her lips. "You *make* your own shear pins?"

"Why don't I take you over to my workshop in the basement. I'll show you my shear pins."

We filled two paper cups with the cheap wine and went out into the crisp evening. I was sure that she'd clean up nicely, and even if she didn't, so what; I'd never run out of things to talk about.

This one DEFINITELY had possibilities.

Biography

Jerry Harju was born in Ishpeming, Michigan, in 1933. He received a degree in engineering from the University of Michigan in 1957 and an MS from the University of Southern California in 1985. After thirty years as a technical manager in the aerospace industry in Southern California, Jerry took up writing as a second career. *Northern Reflections, Northern D'Lights, Northern Passages, Northern Memories,* and his latest work, *Northern Tales No. 5* are collections of humorous short stories and essays about growing up in the Upper Peninsula in the 1930's and '40's. *The Class of '57* takes readers along a humorous and nostalgic path during Harju's six years of "higher education" at the University of Michigan. University life then, with its 1950's attitudes on world affairs, morality, and women's roles in society, was much different from today. *Cold Cash* is Jerry's first novel, a wacky tale about two amateurs who decide to solve their cash-flow problems by pulling a bank heist and getting away on snowmobiles. Typical of Harju's work, the robbery doesn't go as planned and is further complicated by two strong-willed women. *Here's what I think..., Way Back When,* and *Our World Was in Black & White* are selected collections of Jerry's columns that have appeared for several years in the Marquette newspaper, *The Mining Journal.* To respond to fans who have trouble reading, *The Witches Picnic* in a 2 disc set of some of Jerry's classic stories narrated by Ben Mukkala.

Jerry has begun publishing works by other authors. *The U.P. Goes to War* by Larry Chabot has become a local best seller.
In addition to writing books and newspaper and magazine columns and running a publishing company, Jerry travels all over the globe.